Goldsworthy Lowes Dickinson
WHY WE FIGHT WARS

Goldsworthy Lowes Dickinson

WHY WE FIGHT WARS

CAUSES OF INTERNATIONAL WAR
&
WAR: ITS NATURE, CAUSE AND CURE

SPINEBILL PRESS

© Spinebill Press 2022

All rights reserved. Apart from any fair dealing for the purposes of private study, research, criticism or review permitted under the Australian Copyright Act 1968, no part may be stored or reproduced by any process without prior permission. Enquiries should be made to the publisher.

Spinebill Press
Katoomba NSW, Australia
spinebillpress.com

 A catalogue record for this book is available from the National Library of Australia

ISBN 978-0-6455948-0-5

Design and typography by Michel Streich
Typeset in Caslon and Futura

Contents

Causes of International War

1. *The Sense of Community as a Condition of War...* 9
2. *The Origin and Development of War...........* 15
3. *War Between States ....* 23
4. *The Responsibility for War of the Various Elements in a State ....* 49
5. *Remedies ....* 71

War: Its Nature, Cause and Cure

Preface 87
1. *War Means the Destruction of Mankind.........* 91
2. *War Cannot Be Regulated.....................* 93
3. *What Soldiers Have to Do....................* 99
4. *What the Logic of War Approves ....* 105
5. *The Press in Wartime ....* 109
6. *Science and War ....* 115
7. *History and War............................* 119
8. *The Results of War ....* 123
9. *Is War Inevitable? ....* 125
10. *War and Human Nature.....................* 131
11. *The Real Causes of the Great War ....* 135

12 *A Sidelight on the Statesmen of the War*..........151
13 *The Peace* 159
14 *Some Reflections by Mr Lloyd George* 179
15 *The Old Policies Are Still Supreme in Europe*.....185
16 *Why Not Disarm?* 193
17 *The Economic Motives for War* 201
18 *The Issue for the Elector* 209
19 *Economic Principles of a Policy of Peace* 213
20 *Political Principles of a Policy of Peace* 217
21 *The British Empire*...........................225
22 *Conclusion*...................................231

Notes 235
Short Bibliographies............................247

CAUSES OF
INTERNATIONAL WAR

Chapter 1

The Sense of Community As a Condition of War

In discussing war, it is important to distinguish clearly what we mean by it. We do not mean anything so general as conflict or fighting or competition. We mean the deliberate use of organised physical force by groups of men against other groups. Other kinds of conflict might, and no doubt would persist in the absence of war; and to put an end to war would not be the same thing as to put an end to competitive effort. That is clear from the history of states. For within an ordered state there is peace, but none the less there is conflict.

It is necessary, also, for the purpose of this essay, to distinguish international war from civil. In some periods of history, the distinction is not easy to draw in practice. But it becomes clear as soon as sovereign states have appeared. International war is, then, war between such states; while civil war is war between groups included in one of them. More generally, in international war the parties contending do not recognise one another as belonging to a single community; in civil war they do. These two kinds of war have many features in common, but their causes and objects are different. We confine ourselves here to the causes and objects of international war.

War, we must first insist, requires accounting for. For, on the face of it, it is not natural but strange. A quarrel, ending with a fight, between two individuals, everyone understands. The men are angry, and they want to hurt one another. But in war, none of the individuals concerned need be, and in fact, commonly, none of them are, at all angry with one another. They have no kind of personal quarrel. Insomuch that, as is well-known, in the late war, during lulls in the fighting, quite friendly relations were sometimes established between the opposing regiments and "fraternising" had to be prohibited and punished by the officers. Millions of men, for four and a half years, were engaged in killing one another, with every circumstance of cruelty, yet broadly speaking, none of them in any way disliked the others. On the face of it, that is a very curious fact. It is the purpose of this book to enquire how it comes about.

It could not come about (this is the first point we must notice) unless man were, as he was long ago called, a "social animal." But what is meant by being a social animal? It might mean being a herd-animal, like wolves or sheep. Such animals, it is presumed, are united by a special gregarious instinct, not possessed by solitary creatures, and causing them to behave in a quite different way to these. Some think that man is such an animal, and that his coherence in groups depends on such an instinct. Others believe that the earliest men knew no larger community than the primitive family. The question is one for biologists to settle. What concerns us here is that, whatever the origin of the feeling of community, we experience it as something direct and primary, seeming to lie deeper than any reasons we may give for it. The reader may test this by observing himself (or others) when, for example, his family is insulted, or his school, or his country. Most likely he will, in the expressive phrase, "bristle all over," and that quite immediately and uncontrollably, and without respect to the question whether or no the insult is justified by the facts. In such cases, there seems to be touched a kind of extended self, as near and dear as one's own, and near and dear without any reference to its merits. "Good or bad, it is mine, it is me" – that is what something seems to say inside one. That "something" we shall call the community-sense, and we must carry it with us in our minds as a fundamental condition of the possibility of war.

But this sense, whatever its origin, is only a kind of first matter, which receives, from a long course of living together, all sorts of forms. The customs, traditions and history of the group coalesce with it. It supports them, they shape it. An irrational feeling may thus become amalgamated with what is rational and the instinctive movement which rushes to the rescue of "my" group in danger, may present itself as a deliberate preference and choice. Thus, a man may support his instinctive rally to his group by the remembrance of deeds performed in the past by distinguished members of it, of services done to civilisation or liberty, of demonstrable merits of one kind or another, such as a group with a long and continuous tradition is likely to be able to boast. The proportion in which these reflective and rational elements overlie the primitive feeling will differ for different groups, different individuals, and different states of civilisation. The patriotism, for instance, of a cultivated Roman of the age of the Antonines was something very different from the tribal feeling of a Frank or a Hun. But the persistence of the irrational element, even when it is most overlaid, can be detected by an outsider, in the partiality with which the member of a group estimates the excellences of that group in comparison with those of others. Commonly indeed, and in time of war invariably, even to attempt impartiality is regarded as an offence; and "my country right or wrong" is still the maxim of the great majority of patriots. Even those who condemn that attitude do, nevertheless, usually manage to bring out their country as obviously right. The fact that this is always done by both sides in a war shows that something is at work other than a sane objective judgment. That something is what we are calling the community-sense.

We have, next, to notice that, while this community-sense seems to be primitive and persistent, it has not a necessary and exclusive reference to any particular group. It is connected, to begin with, with the groups in which a person is brought up; the family, the village or town, the school, the college, the nation. These various loyalties are not incompatible with one another; on the contrary, they commonly grow up together and coexist harmoniously. They are each the result of habits, customs, traditions and ideas cooperating with the community-sense. But also they may conflict in the most tragic way. When a person marries, for example, there may arise a clash of family loyalties. When one community is conquered by another and annexed, a new loyalty is demanded of it, incompatible with the old. The demand may or may not be met. Centuries of connection have not produced a loyalty of Ireland to Britain. On the other hand, the Boers, whom we annexed by war in 1901, were fighting side by side with us in 1914, and it is probably safe to say that those who thus fought did it as unquestioningly as the British themselves. The community-sense, it would appear, can migrate in the most surprising way. It is, one might say, in itself, nothing more than a permanent possibility of attachment to a group. Most surprising are these migrations when conflict occurs between class-loyalty and nation-loyalty. If a revolution takes place in any country during a foreign war, it often happens that the class dispossessed of power and property makes common cause with the foreign foe. The latter, who, before, were unspeakable enemies of the human race, suddenly become saviours of civilisation; while, on the other hand, fellow-countrymen, a moment ago brothers in a holy war, are transformed into fiends incarnate. We can study this curious phenomenon in ancient Greece, in mediaeval Italy, in the France and the Russia of the revolutions. The nation-group, in such cases, is torn asunder into two class-groups, and these make war upon one another with the passion that is always developed by the community-sense whenever it is challenged by force.

Conflict, it must next be observed, seems to be necessary to evoke the full vigour of the community sense. This may be witnessed in countless instances of daily life. A football match, a boat race, an election, excite a passion wholly irrational and wholly social. The tradition of a school, a college, a club, or even a nation, is something of which the members are very little conscious until it is challenged. A candid judgment, I think, will admit that, in time of peace, patriotism is not a motive for most citizens. They are, no doubt, living within their national tradition, as fish live in water, and would be quite different people without it. But their interest is directed to their work, their amusements, their science or their art. They are pursuing ends that have no conscious reference either to the prosperity or the credit of their country. It is only in war that patriotism becomes, for most citizens, a dominant motive. Similarly, it is only when a social class is threatened that it develops the terrible passions shown in civil war. The community-sense normally lies stagnant. A word may stir a ripple on its surface, but it requires a threat and a blow to raise a storm. And it is only when the storm is raised that we become fully aware what an inheritance we are trailing with us from a far past.

Chapter 2

The Origin and Development of War

We have seen that the community-sense is a condition of the possibility of war. But it is not enough to account for war. There would be no war if there were only one community, and that not sub-divided into smaller groups. But in fact we know of no such condition. Wherever we come across men, we find them grouped in smaller or larger communities each more or less complex within itself, and each in contact with others which it regards as outsiders.

Even so, however, it is not self-evident that outsiders should be treated as enemies. Animals do not make war, pack with pack, on their own kin. Such war, outside mankind, is only known among bees and ants. It seems to be an anomaly in nature, rather than a rule. And it is questionable whether it existed among men during millenniums of their primitive history. Early men hunted animals, but there is no evidence that they fought one another. And whereas Man may have appeared on the earth a million years ago, war, some think, does not go back more than two hundred centuries. There is no evidence for the statement, sometimes hastily made, that whenever and wherever there have been men there has been war. War more likely, came in, as, perhaps, it may go out. It is not a fatal product of human nature. It is an effect of that nature when put under certain conditions.

Nor again does it seem to be true, as is sometimes assumed, that primitive men, even at that late stage of history in which we begin to have record or observation of them, are in a condition of perpetual war. On the contrary, we not uncommonly find small groups living in loose contact, mostly in peace, but occasionally "scrapping" about some definite matter, like the poaching of one on what another claims to be its hunting ground, or the carrying off of a woman. Something like this is the earliest origin we can trace for war. But it is very different from war fully developed. The fighting is unorganised, and it may be carried on not between whole groups but between single families within groups. The battles are anything but bloody, and an actual casualty may terminate the proceedings in general dismay and regret. It is a long step from this kind of primitive quarrel to what history knows as war, and the stages of development cannot be certainly traced in a regular series. But all the known facts suggest that economic motives were at the bottom of the process. For instance, disputes about hunting grounds are a primitive cause of fighting, where different communities are settled in the same neighbourhood. Such causes of dispute are likely to be more common and more serious where tribes in the pastoral stage of civilisation wander far over long distances between their summer and winter quarters, as, for many thousands of years, has happened in the steppes of Asia and Eastern Europe. Disputes of this kind would develop the readiness to fight, and the weapons and tactics of a rude kind of war. But further, under the precarious conditions of this kind of life, a bad season, and the perishing of beasts on a large scale, may leave a tribe face to face with the choice between starving and stealing from others. Hence, wars for subsistence, leading on naturally to the habit of war for plunder. Such wars constitute the greater part of the history of Central Asia. Sometimes this struggle of pasturing hordes led to migration in mass, the defeated being compelled to seek a new country. And these migrations led to attacks on more civilised peoples settled, on an agricultural basis, in more fertile land – in China, for example, or Mesopotamia. It was such migrations that led to the invasions that destroyed the Roman Empire.[1] Quite analogous are the sea-raids that broke up the ancient civilisation of Crete, or those of the northern Vikings. In all these cases, covering many centuries of primitive war, over a great part of the earth, plunder is clearly the motive; and one may say, without much fear of mistake, that that motive is the origin of war.[2] This original motive war carries with it through all its developments. But, later, war was established, as it were, on its own feet, as a normal form of activity, by important social changes. To describe these in detail, would be to rewrite history. But it will be useful to call attention to two main points. First, whatever men do, necessary or unnecessary, good or evil, they put into it intelligence and will. War has been no exception, but rather a principal example. Once the practice of war began, it took on a momentum. On the one hand, an art of weapons and of their use, of tactics and strategy, was developed; on the other, a social attitude and tradition. Those nations became victorious which were able to show the greatest invention in the art of war, the most indifference to killing and being killed, and the strongest and most tenacious acceptance of war as at once necessary and honourable. Innocent savages who burst into tears when they find they have killed an enemy, and run away when they think they may be killed themselves, stand, of course, no chance in such a competition. The settled and civilised peoples of the Roman Empire stood very little chance against the nomad Huns. Nor can the modern Chinese or Africans put up a successful fight against the white race. But the very fact that war has become the subject of an art, is an obstacle to any effective criticism of its necessity or utility. For every art becomes a purpose in itself, and resists and resents discussions that may undermine it. It is not from the makers of bows or spears, of rifles or cannon, of the poison-gasses and disease-germs which are now taking their place, that there could be expected a candid investigation of the value of their own activities. Professional and personal pride forbids it (for what are they, if their calling be discredited?), and so does economic interest. The makers of weapons are not more likely to be tolerant of pacifists, than were the silversmiths in Ephesus of Christians.

Even more important, in the process of converting war from a plunder-raid to an institution, is the development of a special fighting class. The nomads whose activities fill so great a part in the history of war were not professional soldiers. Their wars were episodes in the business of herding their beasts. And though they would sometimes unite in great armies, under some chief of military genius, their social organisation continually tended to revert to small clans of more or less equal freemen. In some cases, however, long periods of fighting and invasion produced the segregation of a special governing and fighting class, whose tradition, occupation, and ideal was all of war. European and Japanese feudalism, so curiously alike, though never in contact, are the great examples of this development. The Teutonic tribes, from the first records we have of them, already have the practice and ideal of war. With that ideal, they invaded the Roman Empire, and in the long process of settling down transformed their whole social organisation in the way best calculated to stereotype the war-like tradition. Chiefs were converted into hereditary kings, their personal followers into lords, and the mass of free men into vassals or serfs. There has now grown up a governing class which is also a fighting class. War is their principal business. They live by and for it, hold their land by and for it, are trained for it and for nothing else. It is their continuing interest that there should be war. And, also, it is their ideal.

They think no other life worthy of a man. When they are not engaged in war, they are playing at it in jousts and tourneys, or talking about it, or hearing it sung about. Finally, all the resources of art and religion are brought to bear to consecrate their life. The warriors are grouped in Orders, blessed by the Church, and trained in the code of chivalry. War has reached its apotheosis. It has passed from being a blind necessity fallen into by primitive and hungry men to being the only purpose of life conceivable for men held to be civilised and noble.

This brief indication must suffice to put the reader on the track of the origin of war and its development. The process may be summed up as the conversion into an institution of what, to begin with, was armed robbery. The armed robbery stage has filled an enormous space of human history, and still continues in certain parts of the world. It hung about the skirts of the early empires in Egypt and Mesopotamia and China. It sent out, from time to time, great swarms of nomads that overwhelmed these empires and settled down on the top of them, again to be overwhelmed by later swarms. Much of such war, however large in scale, did not involve fundamental social transformations among those who carried it on. They remained mere plundering hordes. But there were peoples and conditions where there developed a distinct fighting and governing class, with a tradition and ethic all of war. The feudalism of the European Middle Ages is the best known example. But we find a similar development in Japan, and something in many ways analogous in those Homeric poems which describe war in the Mediterranean region after the break-up of the old Minoan civilisation by invasions from the north. We may call this development the institutionalising of war. And it is important to note that this institutional war preceded and was inherited by the organised states both of ancient Greece and of modern Europe.

It is war between such states with which we in our time are concerned. And our discussion and analysis of that must be fuller than our sketch of its prelude.

Chapter 3

War Between States

By a state is meant a settled population living in an orderly way under an established government. Dimly we see such states growing up in the dawn of history in fertile rivers valleys, the Nile, the Tigris and Euphrates, the great rivers of China; on islands, as Crete; on strips by the sea coast like Tyre and Sidon. Our knowledge of the history of these early states is sketchy; but war is a great part of it; war either with invading nomads from land or sea, or with other states. We may pause for a moment to point out the difference in kind between these two kinds of wars. The first is the repelling of plunder raids; and while states have on their borders unsettled and uncivilised tribes, they will have to wage such war. Modern examples are a frontier war on the north-west border of India, or a war between white settlers and the tribes in the African interior. Such war is only a prolongation of the primitive war dealt with in the last chapter. The essential and characteristic wars of states are those they wage with one another. Such wars might be called classic wars. They are those which fill the history of which we know most; in particular, the history of ancient Greece and of modern Europe.

The transition from the one period to the other may be summarised as follows. Ancient Greece, so tiny geographically, was nevertheless divided into a large number of states. The states were cities, with a little territory round them, about as big as an English county. And though all Greeks were, and recognised themselves to be, of kindred descent, yet these cities were continually at war, and it was these wars that in a very brief space destroyed their independence. After some two centuries of glorious life Greece fell under the domination first of the kingdom of Macedon, and later of the republic of Rome.

Rome too began as a city state, and her history, too, is one of continual war. But the course of it was very different from that of any Greek city. It was one long career of conquest. Rome subdued and brought under her own political system, first her immediate neighbours, then gradually all Italy. She fought Carthage for the empire of the west, and Macedon and Egypt and the princes of Asia for that of the east. She extended her rule over the savage tribes of Gaul and Britain and north Africa till her frontiers at last reached the Rhine and the Danube, Mesopotamia and the mountains of Armenia. For once in its long turbulent history, Western Europe and the Near East rested under a single rule, and cultivated men dreamt of a perpetuity of peace. But this Roman Empire, vast though it was, covered, after all, but a very small part of the eastern hemisphere. Outside, to north and east, wandered warlike tribes. And it was these, breaking through, in the fourth and following centuries, that destroyed the Roman state, without being able for centuries to establish any other. Hence the long anarchy on which we touched in the last chapter. When it subsided, it was not one state that emerged, but, as before in Greece, many states. Renaissance Italy reproduced almost precisely the conditions of that old Greek world. The rest of Europe separated off into larger states under kings, and by the sixteenth century the international conditions to which we are accustomed were already in the main established. Europe was a world of country-states, as Greece had been a world of city states; and Europe, like Greece, was continually at war.

It is this war between states that is specifically meant by international war, which would be better called interstate war. And only when men are definitely grouped into states is the distinction quite clear between civil war and that other kind with which we are here concerned. Interstate war is between states, civil war within states.

But then, why do states wage war with one another? There are not, on the face of the matter, the same causes or reasons for war that we discovered in the last chapter. The communities engaged are settled, not nomad, they live by agriculture and commerce and the arts; they have laws, constitutions, a whole tradition and practice of orderly civil life; they are on much the same level of civilisation; they have many kinds of pacific intercourse; they form alliances with one another; they have (in ancient Greece and in modern Europe) a common religion, a common art, a common literature. They do not habitually live by plundering one another; and if their population becomes excessive they have a recognised practice of orderly emigration and colonisation. Why then should they fight one another? It is not sufficient to say that they have disputes. For disputes need not be adjusted by war, and very often are not, even between states. In the retrospect it appears plainly that it is their interest not to wage war. For the wars between Greek States destroyed the political independence of them all, subjected them first to Macedon and then to Rome, and made their history as brief and tragic as it was brilliant. The wars between the Italian states of the later Middle Ages and the Renaissance resulted, in a similar way, in the reduction of a great part of Italy under a foreign yoke, and the subsidence of what remained Italian into political, intellectual and moral stagnation. And the wars of modern Europe? Well, let the reader look about him and consider. Wars between States clearly need accounting for. Let us try to give the account.

First, then, we must remind ourselves that states, at any rate in the examples of which we know most, have emerged out of earlier conditions, all of war. Thus they carry with them from the beginning both a community-sense directed upon war, and a habit and art of war. They start in as an armed pack, and develop, instead of getting rid of, this original bias. Let us sketch this development.

First, the community-sense, as we have called it,

takes, among the citizens of states, the specific form of patriotism. It would be pedantic and misleading, in a matter concerning feelings, to draw hard and fast distinctions. But broadly, it may be said, with sufficient truth, that patriotism, in its complete development, is only possible in states. The members of a primitive wandering tribe are, presumably, bound together by something much less conscious and elaborate – by an almost animal feeling that they belong together. The vassals of a feudal lord are bound to him by personal loyalty. But the members of a state are united by patriotism.[3]

This patriotism is based upon the primitive community-sense. A common language and religion, common customs and habits give to this sense its local habitation, in which the citizens dwell naturally as in a home. But this feeling of at-one-ness is not yet patriotism. Patriotism is conscious and is inculcated. It depends upon bringing to the mind of the citizen, by whatever educational means present themselves, the past history and achievement of the state. Such history may be true or false, but it must be moving, and movingly presented. Often it has included legends of a common descent from a heroic or divine ancestor. Always it has included stories of war, of danger faced in common and overcome. Patriotism, thus, is bound up with war and religion, and these latter are bound up together. For whatever private religion individuals or groups or churches may profess, the public religion is always one that allows and justifies war, and the official priests of it war-patriots. Further, as has already been remarked, it is especially in time of war that patriotism flourishes. For, first, it is a form of that primitive community sense, which (as we have seen) flames up most fiercely in conflict. And next, its traditions are mainly of war. This connection between patriotism and war the reader may test by the actual history of states. It is in time of war, he will find, that the members most closely hang together. In time of peace class antagonisms assert themselves, often to the point of civil war. Rarely, if ever, has patriotism inspired a social class to abandon important privileges and interests for the sake of the good of the whole community. In Greece this almost never occurred, revolutions there being commonly accomplished by civil war and often with the help of a foreign foe. Rome, in the earlier period of the republic, was wiser and more patriotic, and for that reason succeeded better than any Greek state had done. But even so the principal concessions of patricians to plebeians were wrung by a general strike against war when the foreign foe was at the gate. Broadly it is true that patriotism is a force effective only for war. To say then that the citizens of a state are patriotic is to say that they make war. Whether there might be some community-feeling operative with equal energy in a world at peace, may be matter for speculation. But if there were, it would be something different from what we call patriotism.

Next, we must note that states start as communities of armed men, and therefore as a possible menace to other communities. The importance of this fact cannot be exaggerated. In the first place it creates suspicion. One who *can* attack always *may* attack; and assurances that arms are only for defence will never be convincing. Thus every state will seek to be stronger than others, if only in order to feel safe, and by so seeking will itself become an object of fear to those others. The fear will be proportioned to the menace of the armaments. Under modern conditions, with the perpetual development of new means of offence and the tremendous advantage of a sudden attack on a state insufficiently prepared, the fear becomes so intense that the mere existence of armaments is enough to provoke war. For a state or an alliance of states that thinks itself, for the moment, in an advantageous position is tempted to precipitate the war which all parties regard as inevitable, in order to make sure of victory. Thus armaments, even if they were honestly maintained only for defence, would tend to produce what they are supposed to obviate. And there is no idea more illusory than that still generally held that the best way to avoid war is to prepare for it.

A state, then, is armed patriotism. But it is something more. In relation to other states, it is armed egotism. Its members regard it as a kind of super-person. And the primitive instincts and feelings that centre about real personalities are artificially transferred to it. Its "life" or "existence," men say, is threatened; its "honour" outraged; it is capable of being insulted; it demands "reparation." These metaphors would, of course, have no power if they were not working upon the community-sense heightened into patriotism. But they have also a further significance. Through them individual citizens are able to find an outlet for the primitive emotion which social needs and rules check and thwart in the ordinary relations of life. The state thus becomes an immense reservoir, into which are poured the otherwise balked egotisms of its members. In one sense, it is true, they sacrifice these to the State. But in another, they satisfy them in it. All that an ordered society inhibits – the blow for a blow, the being judge in one's own cause, the exaction of one's own remedies and one's own revenge – all this, repressed in disputes between individuals by the cold arbitrament of justice, comes back a million-fold enhanced when one state deals with others. The duel is forbidden. How much the more delightful, when one's state has been insulted, to send a challenge! Theft is forbidden. How much the more satisfying to steal with impunity from the foreigner! Power over one's fellow-citizens is limited by law. How much the more intoxicating its unrestricted use against the members of another society! And all this, not merely without a bad conscience, but with a good one; approved by oneself, approved by one's whole people! For whatever a state does its members (at any rate, the bulk of them) regard as done justly and righteously. They do not say (unless they be unusually candid and brutal) "We seek power." They say "We seek the Right." They do not say "We seek markets or plunder." They say "We seek to civilise backward populations." They do not say "We are angry and want to hit out."

They say "We have to vindicate our honour." But this honour is always found to be indistinguishable from prestige; prestige from power; power from interest.[4] The state is egotism incarnate, unblushing, proud of itself. And in that huge egotism the citizens find more than compensation for the sacrifice, even it may be to death, of the egotism of their own individualities.

The State being thus not only armed patriotism but armed egotism it is, in fact, generally true that armaments exist as much for offence as for defence. At almost any moment in history, in a political world of states, the student will find that some one or more of these is not merely believed to be, but is, a menace to its neighbours. For it is trying to get something which it can only get by taking it away from others.

What is this object thus pursued by the egotism of states? It is the simplest and crudest conceivable, that which is at the root of all animal life, and which it is the object of human discipline to temper, restrict and divert to higher aims; namely, the maintenance and increase of material power. In an individual, this means the nourishment and growth first of his body, then of his possessions, then of his influence. In the state it means the extension of its territory and of its subjects. There may be, no doubt, states that are, in fact, too weak to pursue this object and yet continue to exist by the grace and self-interest of more powerful neighbours. Such are the small states of contemporary Europe, so hated and despised by Treitschke. These are maintained only because, and so long as, the greater states choose. How precarious such existence is the whole history of the Low Countries shows. Their greater neighbours have always wanted to eat them up, and been restrained only by their jealousy of one another. The same is true of the small states in the Balkans. They have subsisted because, and so long as, more powerful states were not yet ready to test by war which of them should swallow them up. More usually, small and weak states are destined to be brought by force under the power of great ones, as happened, for instance, when Macedon swallowed up Greece, Rome Macedon, Prussia Hanover, Great Britain the Boer republics. The small non-expanding state, preserved under a "balance of power" has been a rare and exceptional phenomenon in history. The rule is that states, all the time, are trying to expand, and either succeeding and becoming empires, or failing and becoming subject, or maintaining a precarious balance of power.

In this competition of states there occur episodically wars "for Liberty." It is important to notice this fact, because it is such wars, and their famous battles – Marathon and Thermopylae, Magenta and Solferino – that connect war with idealism. But there could be no liberation without servitude. Deliverance always postulates oppression, and a righteous war an unrighteous one. The essence of the activity of states is the pursuit of power by violence, the accident is the hit-back of the weaker against the stronger. Of the truth of this the reader may convince himself by noting how commonly in history a nation that has liberated itself sets out immediately to conquer others. For example, no sooner had Athens defeated the Persians than she built up an empire of her own and aimed at the conquest of the Mediterranean world. No sooner had Spain expelled the Moors than she set out to secure the hegemony of the two hemispheres. No sooner had England defeated the Armada than she was knocking at the gates of India and America. No sooner had France become mistress in her own house, than she began to aim at the mastery of Europe. At the moment of this writing examples are before us even more arresting. There is hardly one of the new States called into life by the victory of the Allies that is not coercing under its rule large alien populations and openly aspiring to a career of power. The new Hellas is to be, in the words of its greatest statesman "great and rich and powerful, corresponding to the highest flights of our national aspirations."[5] "I do not fear being reproached for urging force," says a Czech patriot, "for the Czechs were the conquerors and the German Bohemians the conquered who must bear the consequences of their defeat."[6] The new Poland is already making war[7] to recover its former empire, though that comprises more than ninety per cent of non-Poles. All these states have introduced conscription; all are thinking, from the first, not how they may repair the ravages of war and give to their unfortunate people a new and free and prosperous life, but how they may extend their territories by further aggression.

In this complicated process of power-hunting it is

hardly possible to distinguish defensive and offensive action. For any expansion of power may be regarded as defensive, since, obviously, the stronger you are, the less open to successful attack. It is the same principle of insatiability as that which makes men strive continually to increase their fortune. The bigger it is, they feel, the safer they are. They are on an inclined plane, and if they don't move up, they will slip down. So with States. If they are not advancing, they think they will be retrograding. There is usually a great deal of argument, in the case of any given war, as to who was the immediate aggressor. But such argument really is as otiose as it is inconclusive. While States continue to exist in the relations in which they always have existed, they will all be always at once on the offensive and the defensive, except those weaker ones that may be kept in a stationary condition by a kind of vassalage to the powerful.

Now, while these conditions continue, no equilibrium can be other than transitory. For an equilibrium is maintained by alliances and understandings. But these, as all history shows, are temporary and precarious, depending on the relative strength, at any moment, of all the competitors, none of whom is held to its allies by any other principle than that of self-interest, and any of whom may therefore be detachable, if, and when, the conditions of its interest change. The history of states illustrates this throughout, and nowhere illustrates anything contrary to it. Under such circumstances, the only hope of reaching a stable position would be the domination of all the states by one. It was this that Rome achieved, for a period, in the Mediterranean world, and this that Napoleon aimed at in Europe. But the instinct and passion of all states is against this solution, so that, in Europe as in ancient Greece, it has always been defeated. Europe may indeed some day be dominated. But it would have to be by a Slav or Mongol conqueror. There remains the possibility of a permanent union of equals in peace, but without domination. But that possibility presupposes the abandonment of the power-motive by all the states concerned. It is an object of these pages to demonstrate that that abandonment is a necessary condition of peace.

In the universal pursuit of power various motives and objects may be distinguished. Thus, first, you may make war on a powerful rival, frankly because, if you don't destroy him, he will destroy you. The wars of Rome and Carthage are the typical case of this. The world, these states thought, was not big enough for them both; and historians approve and applaud. "*Delenda est Carthago*," and Carthage actually was razed to the ground by the triumphant Romans. It would be foolish, would it not, to enquire seriously whether Rome or Carthage was the aggressor? This Rome–Carthage position was reproduced (in the minds of soldiers, statesmen and journalists) between England and Germany before the war of 1914. When the war broke out Germans compared it to a Punic war; and it was, they thought, only the first of these. The English were more chary of historical analogies. But it was the English who won.

And though they did not reiterate "*Delenda est Germania*" Germans and Austrians must be thinking that their behaviour is much the same as if they had. Not much, it would seem, has changed in the relations between states during the two thousand years of the Christian era.

Apart, however, from direct attack on a rival in order to destroy, it, states may be driven into war by the desire to secure a safe frontier. Classical examples are the Roman Empire and the British Empire in India. The trouble is that no frontiers are final. Rivers are little use. Mountains are not much better; the Alps, for instance, have never served to preserve Italy from invasion, nor the Hindu Kush to preserve India. It may always be, or seem to he, a little safer to descend into the plain on the other side of the Range. To secure your frontiers you must fight a series of frontier wars; and in the end probably swallow up weak buffer states or fighting tribes that lie between you and another empire. Thus, before the war of 1914, by progressive advances from both sides, the Russian and British empires had come into contact across the prostrate body of Persia. Examples abound. Poland has no natural frontiers; she will claim very likely some day that she must advance to the Urals and to Berlin and Vienna. The British in the Mesopotamia they are annexing, have no natural northern frontier. They will try no doubt to get to the Caucasus and the Caspian. Are these manoeuvres offensive or defensive? Your answer depends entirely upon the side of the frontier from which you survey the question. Again, you are a landlocked state, and your access to the sea is at the mercy of neighbour states. These states may indeed put no obstacle in your way. But then, they always could, if they liked, and they sometimes do. Their superior position gives them an advantage in a dispute. And, anyhow, to the patriotic mind, it is intolerable that that great "person" one's state should lie in ignominious dependence on another such person. As well be a slave, cries the natural man. Hence, wars to get to the sea. That such access is not really necessary to the prosperity of a state is shown by the case of Switzerland. No matter! Serbia must have her port. Poland must have her port. They could not "exist" otherwise. And so, Hungary must be cut off from the sea, since she is the vanquished, and German territory be cut across by a Polish "corridor." How promising these arrangements are for the future peace of the world, if current policies and ideas are to continue to prevail, it is hardly necessary to set forth.

Just as landlocked states desire to reach the sea, so do sea-going states desire to control narrow waters, for they want a free passage for their trade and their warships. That is why the British are at Gibraltar, and show no signs of moving from it. That is why the bottle-neck that forms the entrance to the Baltic is of so great concern both to England and to Germany. That is why the Suez and the Panama Canals are of world-wide interest. The control of such waters has been, and may be again, the occasion of wars. Does anyone suppose, for example, that if Spain were strong she would acquiesce in the British control of the straits? We took it by force, and we hold it by force. Again we annexed Egypt, in part at least, in order to have a hold on the Suez Canal. And the building and control of the Panama Canal bid fair, at one time, to involve us in serious trouble with America.

The proceedings we have been considering, imply, of course, the continual annexation by war of new territory. In such cases, is the territory itself part of the object, or only an accidental result in the carrying out of a policy? Such questions are hardly asked by those responsible for the conduct of States. But very often the acquisition of territory for its own sake is the whole object of a war. Territory is desired for various reasons. At times when the State is identified with its ruler, as in the East under its great conquerors or in the West, for many centuries of the Christian era, the ruler annexes territory as a landlord buys up estates. It increases his "property" (for it is so that he regards his kingdom or his empire) and by so doing his sense of power and splendour. Much of human history has been directed by this kind of personal ambition. But, unfortunately, the desire to annex territory is not confined to monarchs and emperors, or we might have got rid of it with their disappearance. Contemporary states still pursue that ambition with an avidity and a determination unsurpassed by any absolute ruler. What are their motives?

One motive is the very elementary one, that they want to increase the number of their conscript soldiers in order to hold what they have, or to acquire more. This motive has been frankly avowed by the statesmen of the country which professes to stand at the head of western civilisation. M. Caillaux, in his defence of his policy at the time of the crisis of 1911, explains that his object, and the object of his predecessors, in their colonial policy, was to redress the weakness of France in Europe by acquiring population and territory in Africa. "The statesmen of whom we have spoken took up once more the policy of ancient Rome, poor in Roman citizens, rich in subjects, supplying the absence of Latin soldiers by Gaulish, Iberian or Numidian legions. Colonial expansion became the complement, or rather the buttress of their general policy. It gave France the material power, the necessary weight required for her affirmations of Right in Europe." [8]

That this really is the point of view of the governing class in France is proved by the fact that, since the war, they have introduced conscription into their African colonies, so that the episode at which all Europe that has a blush left in it is blushing – the occupation of Goethe's home at Frankfurt by black troops – may be taken to be only one illustration of a definite policy. The "civilisation" of natives means, we see, in this case, the conversion of them into conscript soldiers.[9] If France persists in her policy, it will almost certainly be adopted by other states, and especially by Great Britain. We have enormous populations capable of conversion into coloured troops; and if war is to continue we shall no doubt so convert them. So that, in the twentieth century, we may find the world still involved in the old circle – "because we have extended our empire, we must have soldiers to defend it; we must therefore extend it still further, in order to acquire the soldiers." To such madness do false ideas and politics conduct states.

It is not, however, in recent years, the military motive which has been the main one in driving states to acquire territory by force. The main motive has been economic. The development of modern industry has created an ever-increasing demand, in western states, for raw materials, cheap labour to extract them, and markets wherein to sell the manufactured goods. The raw materials lie very largely in Africa and Asia; iron, for instance, in Morocco, oil in Mesopotamia and Persia, rubber in West and Central Africa. The cheap labour is on the spot, once the natives have been turned off the land and prevented from living in any other way than by working at a nominal wage for white masters. The markets are where the natives are, if a demand can be created. Driven by these impulses, the principal European states, especially since the eighties of the last century, have been annexing enormous tracts in Africa and Asia. The consequences of this policy to the native populations belongs to another discussion. What concerns us is, that this was one of the causes, and perhaps the principal cause, of the late war. The notion, true or false, of making greater profit by monopolising the resources of undeveloped countries has taken hold of the minds of statesmen and merchants and manufacturers; so that it has come to seem that the wealth and prosperity of any state depends on the amount of territory it can annex to its own flag, thereby securing the power to exploit it exclusively in its own interest. On that assumption, war is the only issue of the rivalry of states, for whatever one takes, the others, it is thought, lose; and it comes to be regarded as a matter of "life and death" that (let us say) the legacy of the Turkish Empire should fall rather to one's own state than to another.

Hence, at bottom, and in the last analysis, the great war; and hence war after war in the future, if the same ideas are to continue to govern the policy of states. That they do in fact govern them, even after the experience through which the world has passed, is shown by the peace treaties with Germany and with Turkey. The victorious states have pursued, in both cases, a policy of dividing the spoils, and they hardly attempt to make a secret of the fact that a main motive of their annexations is the cornering of economic resources.

Our answer, then, to the question why states make war is, because they pursue political and economic power. The answer is so completely borne out by the whole course of history that it cannot be seriously disputed. But some mitigating and modifying considerations may be adduced, and must be touched upon here.

The process of extending power, it is often observed, is also one of extending "civilisation"; and it is commonly justified, after the event, on that ground. By "civilisation" is meant a state of things better than that which preceded the conquest. And it must be remarked, to begin with, that not all conquests are, in that sense, civilising. Nobody thinks that the conquests of the Huns or of the Turks were. Many doubt whether the conquest of the Roman Empire by the barbarians was. And history, perhaps, will take a different view of the conquest of Africa and Asia by the West from that which the West itself generally takes now. To appraise the good and the evil involved in these great world-events is perhaps beyond any human capacity. It certainly cannot be attempted here in a parenthesis. But what must be said, because it is true and relevant, is, that never has any state made any conquest in order to benefit the people concerned, and not in order to benefit itself. The motives for conquest have invariably been those outlined in the previous pages. Later on, no doubt, a sense of responsibility to the conquered has sometimes developed and much has been done which may fairly be regarded as disinterested, whether or no it has been beneficial. But if, and when, that has happened, it does not affect our analysis. States conquer by war in order to secure or extend their power. If it were otherwise, every state would be as much pleased to see "backward" races being civilised by other states as by themselves. Are they, in fact? Has any state ever looked with satisfaction on the annexation of any territory by another state, even though, according to all the current assumptions, it should be to the advantage of the "natives" concerned to be thus civilised by force? It is not the process of civilisation in general which states admire and approve. It is the process of civilisation by themselves. For each thinks that it alone has the capacity of civilising. The French, at the moment of this writing, are intervening in Syria as a civilising power. The fact that the Syrians are fighting them to escape from that process does not affect them. But they would feel it to be monstrous if the civilising mission should be taken from them and handed over to Great Britain. Great Britain on the other hand, shows no enthusiasm whatever for the process of French penetration. Is that because we do it so well and the French so badly? The French do not think so. And we are hardly good judges in our own cause. We think we are the best civilising power, because we are we, not because of the evidence. Plainly, we are not capable of estimating the evidence impartially; and most of us do not even trouble to know what the evidence is.

"Civilisation" is a result of conquest. On the other hand, "liberation" is the undoing of conquest. And states have sometimes liberated subject populations. That is so. But, in the first place, no state has ever liberated its own subjects, given them, that is, complete political independence. The self-governing dominions of the British Empire may be adduced in contravention of this. It may be said that, if they desired independence, we should have to grant it. Perhaps, nay probably, we should. A leading British statesman recently asserted that we should. But the reply was made, in a prominent liberal newspaper, that it would depend on circumstances. We might acquiesce in the independence of Canada or Australia or New Zealand. But we might fight against that of South Africa. No one can say, and most people will hope that the situation will not arise. But in any case, the example is irrelevant, for the population of the Dominions is not subject. Look, on the other hand, at Ireland. There is a nation that has been rebelling against British rule for centuries past. At this moment we are coercing it by methods not easily distinguishable from those we have denounced so passionately when employed by other states. And no one, with the doubtful exception of the Labour Party, is prepared to give this population independence. The reasons are, partly a division of feeling in Ireland itself, partly the pride of dominion, but more specifically, strategical necessities. In other words, we think it right to govern by force a subject people in order to guard our own safety. Egypt is another case in point. A principal reason why we took Egypt, and will not let it go, is that we may control the route to India. The British State is thoroughly determined never to release a subject population so long as its own power and wealth depend, or seem to depend, on holding that population down. And, of course, all other states are the same. It is only *other peoples' subject nationalities* that states are prepared to liberate, and then only when it seems to be to their own advantage to do so.

Let the reader consider, for, instance, the history of the dealings of the Powers with the Balkan peoples during the past century. As a result of a series of wars all those peoples have won their independence, except so far as some of them are still oppressing populations belonging in race or sentiment to others. And they have won it with the help or acquiescence of one or another of the great States. Nevertheless, if the history be followed in detail, it will be seen that the Balkan agony was prolonged for decades by the jealousies of these states, and their pre-occupation with the balance of power. The Turkish Empire was an estate, upon which all of them were casting covetous eyes and all were afraid of precipitating its fall in a way, and at a time, which would give advantage to a rival claimant. It was this situation that drew out, through long years, the Greek struggle for freedom. Russia was willing to intervene effectively, but France and England feared her intervention. The governments of these states were thinking much more of the advance of Russia in Asia and Europe than of the sufferings of the Greek population. The battle of Navarino was received by both with embarrassment. And their efforts were directed to making the territory liberated as small as possible, for fear the new state should come under Russian hegemony. Later, the same determination to check the expansion of Russia led, first to the Crimean War, then to the British intervention in 1878, and the substitution of the treaty of Berlin for that of San Stephano, then to the long duel between Russia and Austria, which prevented for decades any settlement at all. For all these intrigues and delays the wretched population paid in new massacres and oppressions. And it was not till they took matters into their own hands that they won their freedom, while the protecting Powers looked on. Even then, the rivalries of Russia, Austria and Italy vitiated the settlement, and the great war of 1914 was, in one of its aspects, only the war over the Balkans that had been so long and so vainly postponed.

Next, let us take the case of Italy. Two other states intervened actively to assist the Italians in their struggle for liberation. One was France, the other Prussia. In the case of France it may fairly be supposed that one motive of Napoleon III was a belief in the principle of nationality and a desire to establish it. But not for nothing! If France was to intervene, French power must profit. And France accordingly came off with the booty of Nice and Savoy. On the other hand, the same France, immediately after, did her best to prevent the liberation of Naples from the Bourbon tyranny. In the case of Prussia, no one will accuse Bismarck of idealistic aspirations. It suited him to have Italy to assist him in settling accounts with Austria, and he was willing to pay the price of Italian liberation, in order to mark a step on the road of Prussian aggrandisement, and the unification of Germany. These examples, it will be admitted, do not conflict with our general account of the policy of states.

But, it may be said, at any rate the war of 1914 was disinterested. It was waged, among other things, for the rights of small nations. Among other things, yes! But the other things were the determining ones. For every state that entered the war the primary object was its own security and power. Take, first, the defence of

Belgium. It has been, for centuries, a cardinal principle of British policy to prevent by force the occupation of the Belgian coast by a power that might be dangerous to Great Britain. Hence our intervention. But even apart from the invasion of Belgium we should have gone to war, as Sir Edward Grey made perfectly plain, in order to protect France, to whom, in fact, we were pledged. But this pledge was entered into for our own interest. It was part of the system of maintaining the balance of power.

After their victory, when the victors had it in their power to apply their avowed principle, they took case to apply it only where it would strengthen themselves and their allies, and weaken their late enemies. A great Poland was created, to hem in Germany in the east. A great Yugo-Slavia and Czecho-Slovakia to threaten her on the south. But when the application of the principle of nationality might have strengthened enemy states, then it succumbed to the other consideration, power. Thus, first the four million Germans of Bohemia were forced against their will under the domination of their secular enemies, the Czechs. And, secondly, the Germans of Austria were forbidden to join the Germans of Germany, and condemned by that fact, to the complete ruin in which they are involved, the city of Vienna, for centuries a centre of high civilisation, being condemned to slow and inevitable destruction. All this was done because states, as always, were thinking not of Right, but of power.[10]

Chapter 4

The Responsibility for War of the Various Elements in a State

Historians and others, considering the general facts outlined in the preceding pages, have been apt to regard the whole process as what they call "inevitable." In one sense, of course, everything that has happened was inevitable, since it happened. It may also be that everything is pre-determined. But that is not what is meant when it is said that war is inevitable. What is meant is that no human deliberation or choice can affect the matter, one way or the other. What we have described as power-policies these thinkers describe as the "expansion" of states. They treat this expansion as analogous to that of water when it turns into steam, and think it equally foolish to attempt to check the one or the other. This way of thinking comes from talking always about States and Countries and Nations, and never about men and women. For convenience it is necessary so to talk, but there is an evident danger that the words will be converted into things, and States come to be conceived as kind of super-beings which dictate the conduct of their citizens, instead of being, as they are, a mere result of that conduct. Whatever policies states have ever pursued have been the policies of those individual persons who, at the moment, were acting for the states. These persons, again, have been influenced both by the tradition of what other such persons have done before them, and by the general opinion of the citizens of the state or some of them. The whole matter depends on the views held, the passions felt, and the purposes pursued by a number of individual people. To change policy, is to change those views, passions and purposes. And to say that that cannot be done is to beg the question. In truth the very same people who say it are likely to say, in the next breath, that the whole outlook of the German people was radically transformed by education during the last half of the nineteenth century. Unless we are prepared to assert that no experience and no instruction can have any effect upon the human mind, we cannot deny the possibility of such a change in human motives as may put an end to international war. But if we are to affect these motives, we must know what they are, in whom they subsist and how they are maintained and propagated. In other words we must inquire into the responsibility of different elements in states for the maintenance of that power-idea that leads to war.

This inquiry is very difficult and complicated. What is true of one period of history and of one state will not be altogether true of others. We must confine ourselves here to what is most important for us, contemporary conditions, and among them, to those which are generally applicable to all states.

First, then, there is the responsibility of Governments. It is not sole, but it is chief and primary, and that as much, hitherto, in democratic as in autocratic states. For, whatever the form of government, foreign policy in all countries has been conducted by Foreign Offices, and in secrecy. Nor does there seem to be, at present, in most countries, any desire or intention to alter that arrangement. Even in countries like our own, where ministers and the diplomatic services are nominally responsible to a representative assembly, the permanent officials of the Foreign Office have enormous influence. They have the records, the information, the long experience, the tradition, the prestige, the social connections. They form, taken all together, in all states, a kind of diplomatic International, with the solidarity of a professional class. They spring from the well-to-do; for the Foreign Offices have been jealously preserved for the rich, even where other public posts have been thrown open to competition. Thus, they have associated, since their birth, exclusively with people who have never known what poverty, or (in many cases) what work is. The world outside presents itself to them as a kind of raw material, sometimes inert, sometimes recalcitrant, which it is their natural mission to keep and direct on the accustomed lines. Public opinion, like politicians, is a nuisance to be circumvented. Foreign Policy is the concern of Foreign Offices, and it must be governed by the traditional principles. These, of course, are those of power-policy. The reading of history, at school and university, has already taught the young diplomat that all the history of states, in their relations to one another, is a contest for power, and that it is nothing more. Every record and document in the office, every treaty, every correspondence, confirms that view. Every conversation with official superiors presupposes and reinforces it. Every step taken is an example, every despatch an admonition of it. The world to whose inmost secrets the aspirant is gradually introduced, is one where no other view of affairs is even conceivable. The material with which diplomats deal is armed competition. Secrecy and intrigue is the atmosphere they breathe. Or, if they come out into the open, to bargain or to threaten, what they offer, in friendship or hostility, is always an army and a navy. These are the cards without which they could not play their game. So that war, sooner or later, is the presupposition of their whole activity.

They may, of course, and very likely often do, in a general and abstract view, consider war to be an evil. But they are bound to regard it as an evil inevitable; as indeed it is, granted the situation they at once suffer and create, and the assumptions within which their whole life and thought moves.

But an evil believed to be inevitable is one which must not be too particularly contemplated. For at any moment it may be necessary to precipitate it on the world, and one must be sure to have the nerve to do this with courage. It is better, therefore, while admitting that war is an evil, and, of course, doing what is reasonably practicable to obviate it, for as long a time as is possible or convenient, not to let oneself dwell upon it. But, not dwelt upon, it becomes, to diplomats, as to the general public, a mere word without real content. And even when it breaks out and reveals itself for what it is, since these gentlemen do not go to the front, since they do not really bear and suffer war, as the millions must do whom they have flung into it, they are not unduly disturbed, when all is over, by the price that has been paid. Has their country been defeated? Well, that was the soldiers' fault. Has it been victorious? How well, then, the diplomats must have planned! The infinite unimaginable suffering, the degradation of all life, the economic ruin, the setback of progress, the plain fact that nothing whatever has been gained to compensate for all these losses, all that drops out of the mind, because it has never been assimilated by it. The great game has been played once more, and the board is to be set for a new contest. It is the business of the diplomat first, in the peace settlement, to make the situation as favourable for his own side as possible, and then to play the old game with a new skill. The vanquished, with good luck and brains, may recover their position. The victor must try to maintain his. That is all. The tradition emerges unbroken and, really, in the minds of these men, unchallenged. If the reader have any doubt of this, let him consider the series of treaties, all made in close contact and consultation with the diplomatic class, made during and after the great war to end war. Let him examine, carefully and impartially, the presumptions underlying them.

He will see, to demonstration and beyond all dispute, that the territorial and economic arrangements have been dictated by the principle of Power, and that a few score men, working in the dark, have been able in cold blood, and (no doubt) with a perfectly good conscience, to defeat the hope and aspiration for permanent peace of the millions who have died, and the millions who remain to mourn them, to doff aside as an idle dream the cause for which the masses gave their lives, and to reinstate themselves, their hopes, their fears, their ambitions, their unbeliefs, as the governing factor in an international life arranged to lead, as before, to a fresh and even more terrible catastrophe. And, let it be understood, all this has happened not because these are bad men. Most likely they are good and conscientious men. They are, at any rate, what would commonly be thought "nice" men, cultivated, charming, dilettantes of literature and art. Yes! But they are imbued, not through their own fault, with a false tradition and they have never been close enough to reality to correct it. It is impossible for such men to make a good peace, for they are incapacitated from believing in peace.

Or will it be urged that nobody wanted a better peace? This is palpably untrue. For the Labour organisations of every country, during the war and after the armistice, had put forward definite proposals for a peace on quite other lines. They had asked for real self-determination for all oppressed nationalities. They had asked for no annexations and no indemnities. They had asked for a true League of Nations, in which all states should be, from the outset, included. Does any one doubt that, if a congress of socialists had made the peace, it would have been a different peace? As it is, not a single representative of the working class was present at the Peace Conference. They, with their desires and hopes, were simply brushed aside. They were good enough to win the war. They were not good enough to make the peace. That was reserved for prime ministers, acting under the pressure of the great interests, and for the diplomatic class.

The diplomatic class, however, does not work alone. Powerful sections of society have access to it, and exchange with it influences and ideas. Partly, these are the men of the same social class, the same school and college, those who constitute what is called in a special sense "society." All these are naturally solid together, and breathe, and create by their breathing, a single atmosphere. But society is always politically powerful, so that the diplomatic class is always well supported in the political world.

Next, and belonging to the same social class, are military and naval officers. The importance of these men in determining policy differs in different states. Probably it was greatest in pre-war Germany, and least in pre-war America. But wherever it is important, and in proportion as it is important, it must make for the perpetuation of war and of the policies that lead to war. For, in the first place, if a man has trained himself for war, he must, if he be serious and competent, desire to put his training into practice. For otherwise, what is the use of his life? Professional soldiers and professional sailors are, almost by definition, men who believe in war; believe, that is, that it is inevitable, that it is a fine profession and therefore that its evil cannot outweigh its good. To say this, is to attribute no iniquity to this class. Hindenburg, no doubt, and Ludendorff, along with their less prominent and uncompromising fellow-professionals in all countries, are good fathers of families, good patriots, brave, powerful and determined men. But the more they are all that, the more fatally are they opposed to the whole conception and ideal of a world at peace. When Moltke said "Perpetual peace is a dream and a bad dream," he expressed the thought of every good soldier and sailor.

Professional officers, then, like professional diplomats, accept war as a necessary part of the system of things. But there is an important difference in the outlook of the two classes. The soldiers and sailors have actually to conduct both war and the preparation for it. They are thus brought continually into contact with the facts which the diplomats are able to ignore. They are bound to know what war really means, for they are giving it its meaning. Thus it is impossible for real soldiers and sailors to have any of the romantic illusions about war that take the place of experience and imagination in the minds of civilians. It is thus possible for these men to have a conversion – that is, to come to see that war is a thing so evil that nothing can justify it, and that if society does not destroy it, it will destroy society. During the great war we have actual record of such conversions. One, for instance, is the German General Montgelas, selected by a peculiar irony, as one of the "War criminals" by the allied Governments. Another is the naval Captain Persius. Another is the French General Verraux, And it might be possible to add one or two famous English names. If the terrible experience through which he must pass does manage to penetrate to the mind and heart of a soldier, he becomes, of all pacifists, the most convinced. For he has known and felt as no other has.

But this does not very often happen. And for reasons. It is the first business of a professional officer not to let it happen. For if he allowed himself to realise and to feel what it really is to which his life is devoted, he would have to abandon his profession. His instinct, therefore, is to turn away deliberately from all such thoughts. And this, not only in war time, but in time of peace, when, of course, it is much easier. He thus becomes a dual nature. On the one hand, he retains the ordinary habits and feelings of civilian life. He would not hurt a child. He is all good nature, kindness and helpfulness. On the other hand, he is training himself, and other people (and that is his real business) to inflict cruelties unimaginable on innumerable people unknown to him, not men only, but women and little children. For, as he well knows, modern war makes no distinctions of civilian or soldier, age or sex. If he is in the air force, it is his work to accustom himself and others to the notion of dropping bombs into the midst of a helpless herded crowd.[11] If he is a gunner, the tank preoccupies his mind and (like a recent expert on the subject) he contemplates a civilian population (whom he supposes to be "demanding war") "killed in a few minutes by tens of thousands." For the next war ("inevitable" of course) is to open with attacks "not against the enemy's army, but against the civil population, in order to compel it to accept the will of the attacker." Chivalry, mercy, a fair fight, all the apparatus of romance which still does duty among schoolboys, and is still served up, on occasion, in literature, or the cinema, or the press, all this the modern soldier knows to be nonsense. He knows that war means the greatest and most indiscriminate massacre possible of whole populations. He knows that no rules or conventions, even if such be drawn up, will ever be observed. He knows that victory will be to the most unscrupulous, the most pitiless, and the most ingenious. He knows that it is his duty to be that kind of man, and to create that kind of man. He knows that, if he stop for a moment to consider what this is that he is doing, to confront his professional with his private life, he is ruined. Thus, he has to arm himself against his own humanity and his own common sense. He has to regard the responsibility for war as resting elsewhere than on himself, and the fact that it is elsewhere taken as freeing him. He has, in a word, to view himself not as a man and a citizen, but as an instrument of destruction, and thus to make himself immune against the only energy that can extirpate war from the world, namely intellect prompted by humanity. For all this he may, as men choose, be admired or pitied or pardoned. What is said here has not been said in judgment. It has been said to bring out the fact that to maintain an officer class is to maintain a class of men who cannot work against war, and must work for it, unless they undergo a conversion that would shatter their whole life. So that here, once more, we come back, by a new route, to the indisputable fact that to prepare for war is to perpetuate war. An army is not merely a military machine, it is an educational machine, and the object of its education is to extirpate from the minds and hearts of men any feelings and ideas that work against war, to reverse the motives and habits of civilian life, and to sterilise the mind against all influences which might countervail its training in scientific slaughter. Whether an army can effectively do that, or how effectively, may be open to question. That it is its object to do it, may be ascertained by anyone who will inquire into the methods adopted by the sergeants who drill raw recruits, or will turn over the pages of military handbooks. In peace time, it is true, this education is afterwards more or less counteracted, in the rank and file, by their necessary withdrawal into civilian life. But for the professional soldier there is nothing to counteract it, and whether he be admired for the fact or whether he be condemned, he can hardly escape becoming a permanent obstacle to any possiblity of improvement in human civilisation.

Yet bad though the case of these men be, through the obligations of a profession which they may have chosen from the best of motives, it is yet better, in one way, than that of the politicians in time of war. For these have to maintain the cant, "We will not sheathe the sword" they say, and they must say it. For it would never do to say what would be the truth, "We will not cut off the poison gas, nor the bombs on undefended towns, nor the liquid fire, not the lice, nor the typhus, nor the dysentery, nor the slow starvation, by blockade, of millions of women and children." No, the fiction must be kept up! But what a fate is that of those who must keep it up!

To the classes thus directly responsible for the maintenance of war and war-policies must be added some great business interests. This, however, is a very complicated matter to disentangle. Trade and commerce, as a whole, do not profit, but lose, by war, and, in a general way, they are aware of that. Most likely what is called international finance works in the direction of peace, so far as it works at all in politics; and some patriots are its enemies precisely for that reason. And though, no doubt, in time of war, certain industries make enormous profits, yet it would be unreasonable to suggest that they promote war in order to profit by it. On the other hand, there is at least one business which requires war, or, at any rate, the constant menace of war, to thrive at all, and that is the armament business. This business, therefore, has every motive of self-interest to work for war and against peace. It is internationally organised, so that shareholders in every country are making profits out of the munitions destined to be used against their own sons, and its existence has now been formally declared, in the Covenant of the League of Nations, to be "open to grave objections."

But it is in the economic expansion of states that business interests play the most questionable part. The main motives here have been already referred to. Capital wants an investment that will pay a high return; manufacturers want raw material and markets; concessionaires want cheap labour. And all these things they hope to find in countries economically undeveloped and unprotected by strong governments. The hope is not unreasonable, and is sometimes justified by the event. A great deposit of iron, of coal, of gold, of oil, or whatever it may be, taken for nothing by force from primitive populations who do not know its value, may easily bring in high dividends to shareholders. Native populations, driven off the land and sufficiently taxed, may be compelled to give their labour at very low rates. They may possibly even be induced to "demand" European manufactured goods, and to abandon their own handicrafts. Thus, any given set of financiers or manufacturers or traders may really see and find profit in the seizure of African territories or in the opening up by force of Asiatic markets and resources. We should expect therefore to find that schemes of expansion are favoured not only by soldiers and imperialistic politicians, but by business interests. And in fact the history of expansion shows that that is usually the case. It is curious, even before the modern era, to note how trade and markets have always been a main motive of British wars, and a main cause of such popularity as those wars have achieved. But, during the last half century, this motive has been peculiarly prominent. And the combination of the respectable peer, the Company promoter, the trader, the adventurer and the soldier has been behind the colonial enterprises of all countries from the eighties of the last century onward. The career of Mr. Cecil Rhodes is the classical example; for in him were blended all the motives which lie behind empire – patriotism, cupidity, adventure, and the passion for domination and power.

The trouble, of course, is that this expansion cannot take place without war. It implies, first, war upon the natives. For however cunningly they may have been deceived into the grant of concessions, the time comes when the mask must be thrown off, and it must be made plain to them that they are to lose their lands, to abandon their traditional way of life, and to become workers in a semi-servile condition under white masters. That, however, it may be said, is a negligible matter. These native wars, after all, do not cost much, except to the natives, and if that were all it might plausibly be maintained that empire pays. Unfortunately, all states are playing the same game, so that friction is bound to arise. The friction may be allayed for a time by compromises and concessions. But it adds a main contribution to the universal rivalry of power; till, at last, all is put to the stake in a great war, as a result of which the victor takes away the colonial territory of the vanquished, by way of "compensation" or "punishment."

At this point, has empire "paid" or no? Perhaps, after the late war, and its results, no one will have the audacity to answer the question in the affirmative, so clear is it that every nation individually, and all nations taken together, have lost, even in material values, infinitely more than there can be any reasonable hope that even the victors can ever regain. Statesmen and nations, if they mean to be good accountants, must set against the meagre profits of economic expansion, the whole of their war expenditure during the period of expansion. And a mere glance at the finance and trade of colonial dependencies shows how enormous the deficit must be.[12] Although, however, on pecuniary balance, the nation loses, beyond all computation, given interests and individuals may gain. It may therefore be expected that, so long as present policies continue, there will always be, behind schemes of expansion, financiers and business men, and the activities of such men must be reckoned in among the forces working for war. If men could or would think things through, from the beginning to the bitter end, it would be seen clearly that the profits made by these enterprises are made out of the life-blood of the sons of those who engaged upon them. But not so do men think, nor so feel. And it would be unjust to lay upon these patriotic-feeling expansionists the condemnation that would rest upon them if they knew what they did.

We see then that the tradition of the diplomatic class, the professional attitude of soldiers and sailors, and the pecuniary interest of certain business men, work together to maintain the pursuit of power as the policy of states. These classes and interests form a kind of social block, moving in the circle of their own ideas, and permeating one another with them. They may be called, collectively, the governing class. It is not a class whose membership is fixed. New men constantly rise into it, and others go out. But what is, or has been, fixed, is the point of view – power and wealth the object, war, in the last resort, the instrument. It is this governing class that forms policies and carries them out behind the scenes, admitting the Public to its confidence, or to so much of it as seems desirable, only at moments of crisis when passions must be played upon and the people brought upon the stage. This "people," the great mass, that is, of the uninitiated, who pursue their daily work and play, until the trumpet of doom blows from the heaven of their rulers – these must be regarded as victims and dupes, not accomplices, in the great game. But though that be so, yet the masses must bear their responsibility, seeing that it is their passions, instincts and emotions that respond to the call when it is made. The whole state of mind of the crowd is one of the fundamental causes of war.

And, first, we must note that in the crowd must be included the majority of the educated and well-to-do. Very few people take any interest in foreign policy; very few even attempt to follow it through its underground channels or to infer its course from the chance emergence of the stream at this point or that. Most people therefore, educated or no, are, in this matter, a mob. They follow passion not reason, sentiment not interest, words not things. We come back here upon what we have called the community-sense, undiluted, uninstructed, unenlightened by reason or by knowledge. Unable to direct itself, it follows the direction of its leaders, and these are members of the governing class, acting through the platform and the press. For information, and (what is equally important) for the way in which information is presented, the crowd is at the mercy of these influences. It is governed by words; and the words serve not to express and inform thought, but to release passion. It matters little whether or no what is said is couched in the form of a logical argument. Some readers demand this, others do not. But, if argument be supplied, it is passion that dictates both the premises and the conclusions. For once a crisis has broken out between nations, it becomes an axiom on each side, that the other nation is in the wrong. Some want reasons why it is in the wrong, most do not. But no one wants or will tolerate reasons why it may be right. The colossal egotism of the herd at this point takes charge, and any reasoning that can gain a hearing is but sophistry to justify that.

This analysis is not refuted by the fact that nations, in such crises, are capable of generous emotions as well as of the reverse. Egotism can always be generous, when it is contemplating the victims and the crimes of an enemy. What tests it, is its own victims and its own crimes. The very same passion which transports a people at war with fury at the iniquities of its enemies, is turned at once against a candid friend who may seek to expose those of itself or its allies. The righteousness of a nation is self-righteousness. And though it prefers (like all egotists) to cover up its emotions in fine-sounding words, it will never allow idealism to divert it from the course of its own interest and desires. All this is so instinctive that it would be unjust to charge it to hypocrisy. For hypocrisy implies deliberation and self-control, and here all is primitive passion. The inconsistencies between the words of nations and their deeds, between their avowed intentions and their actual accomplishment, between what they profess in conflict, and what they do in victory, runs through the whole course of history. If the reader requires particular illustration, let him compare the declarations of the allied nations during the war of 1914, with their action in the treaties they dictated to vanquished foes.

It would be idle to blame men for having this kind of mind and soul, which they inherit from the animal world. But it is, at bottom, because they have it that wars are possible. For the people, after all, are the great reservoir of force, and governments can only act by and through them. One might compare nations to patients liable to outbreaks of homicidal mania, but normally sane, kindly, helpful and productive. Certain words, rashly spoken, are known to bring on the attacks. Wise and humane keepers would, therefore, avoid speaking them. But the keepers of nations – governments and governing classes – forget or despise this counsel. In thoughtlessness, in misconception, in ambition, in fear, or, it may be, in wickedness, they speak the words. The catastrophe follows, and the patients, falling upon one another, fight till they drop. Bled to sanity, at last they rise heavily from the dust, to lead again, if they may, the human life. But still the old poison is working in them, the old keepers watching and waiting. And when the word is spoken again, once more they will be at one another's throats.

It follows, from the situation thus described, that a government can always reckon on the support of the people for a war, once the war can be presented as "inevitable." It follows also that it will be very difficult for them to make a good peace, even if they want to, and very easy to make a bad one. For though the mass of the people, in every nation, may, in a general way, desire a settlement which will prevent future wars, yet they are neither instructed about the conditions necessary to the attainment of such a peace nor ready to sacrifice to it the passions engendered by war. A victorious nation may want a good peace. But it wants, still more revenge and indemnity. And it does not see that it is precisely the taking of those things that makes future wars inevitable. When the British electorate, in December, 1918, voted for the Kaiser's head and the cost of the war, they voted away the possibility of a good peace.

They were, of course, less guilty than the politicians who seized the most critical moment in our history and in the history of the world, to lay such policies before them. They hoped, no doubt, and intended to have, nevertheless, the peace that would end war. But, if not guilty, they were none the less responsible. For it was their passion, their confusion of mind, their ignorance, their impatience, their refusal, all through the war, to listen to cold and wholesome truth, that encouraged politicians to approach them in that spirit and discouraged them from approaching them in any other. They have been duped, no doubt, they have been cheated, they have been betrayed. Yes! By their governments! Yes! But also by their own passions.

The passionateness, then, of the mass of men in their dealing with other nations, their falling back at once on the blind community-sense, is a principal part of their responsibility for war. Perhaps not less contributory is their levity. When war is over, all they want is to forget it. Instead of taking the opportunity, when the tension and strain is past, to look back in cold blood on all that has occurred, to trace causes and effects, to estimate evils and goods, they put all that behind them and turn to pleasure, to business, to domestic politics, to anything rather than learning the lesson of the experience through which they have passed. That this is natural does not alter its significance, nor obviate its consequences. Until men can learn by experience there is little hope that they will ever emerge from the vicious circle of unnecessary war and unstable peace. We have before us, at this moment, such a lesson as has never been given to the world before. We have seen prodigies of sacrifice, miracles of courage, unimaginable depths of suffering and heights of devotion; we have seen a prodigality and riot of the best and the worst that is in man; and all this goodness and all this badness we have seen directed to internecine destruction in the name of certain abstract principles. Those who stood for the principles have won. They have had power to do what they liked with the world. Triumphant force has been given a free hand to see what it can do to establish Right. What is the result? A scene of ruin, an orgy of hatred, a debauch of cupidity, a deployment of hypocrisy unequalled by anything yet presented in the tragic annals of mankind. These are the fruits of war. Nor will any devotion nor any heroism on the part of those fighting ever cause the fruits to be other. Have we learned the lesson? Do we even know that the lesson is there to be learned? No! We are jazzing, and racing and mobbing Mary Pickford.

Chapter 5

Remedies

This essay is concerned with the causes, not with the cure of international war. But a comprehension of the causes is important only because it is a condition of the cure. A few concluding words may, therefore, be appropriately devoted to remedies.

These fall under two heads; the creation of judicial and administrative machinery, and the adoption of a new outlook and policy. These must go together, if either is to be effective. But the latter is more important, and more difficult, than the former. The machinery, indeed, has already been created. That is the one good work of the Peace Conference. And as, in previous pages, I have had occasion to speak in condemnation of the statesmen there assembled, so I would here pay a full tribute to them for a great achievement. In creating the League of Nations, they showed themselves far-sighted, pacific and humane. If and when the states at present excluded are admitted to the League, if and when it is permitted to take the place at present occupied by the Supreme Council, it will have the opportunity of constituting, maintaining and developing a world at peace.

But a League of Nations of which the component

States should be pursuing the old power-policies would be a contradiction in terms. The creation of the League is nothing, and worse than nothing, unless the governments and the peoples who support them are to be directed by a new spirit. And there is little evidence at present that such a spirit is at work among those who are actually controlling affairs. The governments of all the great states are still pursuing imperialistic policies, as though the League did not exist, and where these policies are concerned, they refuse to let the League function. Thus, when Poland attacked Russia in April, 1920, a case had arisen of the kind contemplated by article 11 of the Covenant. It was the clear duty of the Council of the League to take action. No action was taken, for the principal allies did not desire action to be taken. And they did not desire it because Poland was their ally, and because powerful elements in their own governments had been actively supporting the Polish offensive. The Covenant of the League constitutes a solemn international obligation. Yet already the states that profess to stand for international right have infringed its spirit, if not its letter. Some organs of the press indeed assume, as a matter of course, that the Covenant must be ignored, if it is inconvenient to the signatories to observe it. Thus the *Temps*, that representative exponent of cynical imperialism, when Persia appealed to the League for protection against alleged aggression by Russia (June, 1920) argued that the League should decline to act, because its principal members would not think it worth while to take risks for Persia. Yet Persia is a member of the League and entitled by Treaty to its protection.

Let us take another example of the dealings of the principal Allied States with the Covenant. No article in that document is more important than number 22, which deals with the system of mandates. The intention of this article is to convert annexations of territory by the victors in the late war into mandates held under the League. The territories in question are to be held in trust for the "well-being and development" of the inhabitants. The intention of the article is plain. The mandatory State is to look after the interests of the population entrusted to it, not after its own. It follows that it should not seek pecuniary or material benefit for itself. Its trust is to be a burden, not an advantage. It might therefore be supposed that there would be no great competition for the post of mandatory, and that the obligation would be assumed reluctantly as a duty, not covetously, as an opportunity. What has happened?

Let us take the case of the Turkish Empire. By the Peace Treaty the Turks are to be deprived of the greater part of their territory. How has it been disposed of? According to Treaties drawn up during the war, before the mandatory system or a League of Nations was heard of, and conceived frankly on the old imperialistic lines. The mandates are being assigned to the States by themselves, not by the League, and they themselves are drawing up the terms of their own trusteeship. Britain is to have Palestine and Mesopotamia, France, Syria and Cilicia, Italy, Adalia, and so on. And no concealment is made of the fact that, in all these territories, what interests the self-appointed mandatories is the material resources involved. Why, for instance are the British taking Mesopotamia? From a disinterested desire to benefit the Arabs, our paternal care of whom we are showing, at the moment of this writing, by killing them with bombs and machine guns?[13] He must be very credulous or very ignorant of the ways of states who can believe it. It is not even strategical considerations that move us; for if it were, we should be content to hold the head of the Persian gulf, as we had arranged to do by the Treaty with Germany, drawn up in 1914. No! The lure is the oil. We are, indeed, told that this oil is to belong to the Arab State. But that is "subject to any arrangements that were made before the war with Turkey." And before the war, Turkey had granted a concession of all of the oil of Bagdad and Mosul to a British Company. The ownership of the Arab State presumably will be confined to the power of taxing the company to pay for the administration.

One reason then, we may fairly say, why we are taking Mesopotamia is that a British Company may exploit the oil.

But here there is involved a yet more important point. According to the Covenant, the conditions of a mandate are to be such as will secure "equal opportunities for the trade and commerce of other members of the league."[14] In the case of the Mesopotamian oil, that would imply that neither the British Government nor British subjects would be granted any differential opportunity for the purchase of the oil, either in matter of price or in matter of prior claim. It may be that that position will be maintained by the British Government. But we have reason for anxiety. For, in another case, the government has already adopted the contrary policy. Among the territories for which the British have granted themselves a mandate is a little island in the Pacific called Nauru. This island is rich in phosphates, and, according to the spirit, if not the letter, of Article 22, these phosphates should be offered on equal terms to all nations members of the League. What in fact has happened is, that the sale of the phosphates is to be restricted to the United Kingdom, Australia and New Zealand, unless there be any surplus over and above what they require; and that these countries are to have the right to receive them at cost price. Here, is a clear case of economic imperialism of the worst kind. A territory is seized by war and then the political power of the State seizing it is employed to give that State a preferential claim on its principal raw material, so that it can either exclude all other nations altogether, or charge them a monopoly price. Such a policy is a war policy. For it shows every State that its only security for access to materials is to seize and occupy the territory where they are to be found. It was the clear intention of the mandatory system to put an end to such practices. And here is a British Government introducing them, for the first time, into the British system. The precedent of course will be imitated elsewhere. A coach and four has thus already been driven through one of the most important Clauses of the Covenant. The whole affair is disreputable. But perhaps its most disreputable feature is the speaking in support of the government in the House of Commons. Member after member rose in his place to declare, in effect, that he regarded the solemn international treaty constituting the League as a scrap of paper. One even went so far as to emit the following sentence, worth recording as an example of the political morals of Empire. "On the matter of the League of Nations I think it (the Bill) is a violation of the Covenant, but on the ground of imperial needs, and the necessity for procuring this tremendous and vital product, I shall be inclined to support the government."[15]

And these are the people who professed to the world that they were fighting, a "war for Right."

Oh! young men dead in your millions, for what then and for *whom* has your blood been shed!

It will, perhaps, be said, in extenuation, that this business of oil and phosphates has been exaggerated, and that after all the real concern of the States that are giving themselves mandates is with the interests of the native populations whom they are to protect. Well, this contention can be tested by a typical case, that of Armenia. Here, if anywhere, the conditions contemplated by Article 22 exist. Here is a population which has been decimated by massacre again and again. A million were exterminated by the Turks during the war, and the Allied nations made it a special charge against the Germans that they did not intervene effectively to prevent it. Well, Turkey surrendered to the Allies. They could have made any terms they liked about Armenia. They could have insisted on its evacuation by the Turkish troops, and have occupied the whole territory by their own. But their interests lay otherwhere, in those regions which they had marked out for economic exploitation. The British withdrew from Cilicia, because that province had been assigned to the French by the agreement. The French occupied it, willingly enough, for they had economic interests there. But they had none in the rest of Armenia, which is poor in natural resources, and they did not extend their occupation thither. Massacres recommenced almost under the eyes of the French troops, who seem to have attempted no effective resistance, and who, at the moment of this writing, are withdrawing altogether, leaving the Armenians at the mercy of the Turkish nationalists. Meantime, no mandate has yet been accepted by anyone for these unhappy people. With characteristic cynicism the Supreme Council offered it to the Council of the League. That Council replied in the only way it could. It suggested that it would endeavour to find a State to undertake the mandate, but that it would be glad to be informed what forces and funds would be at the disposal of such a state. Thereupon the Supreme Council, with elegant irony, offered the mandate to the United States. "We have distributed among ourselves" they said, in effect, "all the lucrative parts of the Turkish Empire. There remains Armenia, a territory whose protection will require a considerable expenditure of men and money, and from which unfortunately no return can be expected. We ourselves require all the troops and resources we can afford to protect our oil and other material interests in the late Turkish Empire![16] We have done all we can. It is now your turn to assume your responsibility to humanity." This agreeable offer the Americans unaccountably declined. And the mandate for the Armenians is still to seek. Perhaps before it is found, there will be no Armenians left to enjoy it.

So much for the "sacred trust for civilisation" contemplated in Article 22. There is nothing wrong with the Article. What is wrong, is the spirit of the Allied Governments, and of the classes and interests that dictate their policy. After the war, as before it, these are inspired by economic imperialism of the crudest kind. And while that is the case, the Covenant of the League can never be anything more than a piece of solemn hypocrisy. But of this economic imperialism Great Britain is a principal exponent. There has been much talk in England of Italian and French Imperialism. Fiume and the Saar Valley have bulked large on our horizon. But how little has been said of our own appropriation of East and West German Africa, of Palestine and Mesopotamia, not to mention the protectorate of Egypt, and what will certainly be a hegemony over Persia and Arabia. All that we took quietly, as if it were a matter of course. And what case had we, then, to protest against the more moderate imperialism of other states? They would only have laughed at us, as perhaps they did. Let us admit the truth. Above internationalism, above peace, and at the cost of war, all that is powerful in England values the continued expansion of the British Empire. If ever there were a people who might fairly be accused of making a bid for world dominion, that people is the British. Now, let it be clearly understood, the continued expansion of the British Empire is incompatible with the peace of the world. For it can only be expanded at the cost of other Empires, that is by war. If a League of Nations is to be a reality, the ideal of Empire must disappear, and its place be taken by the opposite ideal – the peaceful co-operation of all states and nations in the interests of a common world-civilisation.

But this conclusion is unwelcome, if not intolerable to the governing classes of all nations, and not least to that of this country. Their tradition, their education, their pride, their interest, all work against it. The imperialism of the wealthy and aristocratic sections of the English, of the army, the navy, the church, the public schools, to a great extent the universities, is so direct, so simple, so unamenable to discussion and argument, as to resemble an instinct. There is no evidence that the war has done anything to it, except to enhance it. As to the League of Nations, these classes either are frankly hostile to it or they regard it as a device to consolidate the Empire by stabilising the status quo after it has been made as favourable as possible to British power. While that kind of spirit animates governing classes, the League simply cannot function.

It is the sense of this irreconcilable hostility of the governing class to the only conditions that can give us a world at peace that is leading so many people to turn, for their only hope, to Labour. A hope, it is, but not a certainty. For, as we have noticed in a previous chapter, the passions, good and bad, of the peoples, make them easy dupes of imperialism. Their leaders indeed, in all countries see the truth clearly. But it must be doubted whether the rank and file do. A great work of education has here to be done. Internationalists must contend with imperialists for the mind and soul of the peoples. Imperialists have at their disposal the money, the press, the innumerable agencies of corruption and intrigue. Above all they have, if they choose, one great bribe to offer. They may go to the working class and say: "We offer you a tribute Empire. Black men, yellow men, brown men, shall slave throughout the world to give you cheap raw materials. We will share the spoils with you – honestly, we will! We will all grow rich together at the price of their poverty. Let us stop this idle wasteful fighting with one another. Let us join hands to exploit our subject peoples." Of course, it is not thus that it will be put. But its cynicism, its folly and its wickedness will not prevent its being put in some more plausible form. Before the working people are secured for internationalism, they will have to stand up against a deadly assault of imperialism upon their predatory instincts.

Nothing will enable them to resist such an assault except education. But how is that education to be given? It is natural to think, in this connection, of the public educational system, of the schools and colleges maintained or assisted by the State. But there are difficulties here. There is no greater danger to democracy than a deliberate system of governmental education in morals and politics. It might, indeed, be used for good, but equally and more probably, it might be used for evil. It seems essential to liberty and progress that such subjects either be not taught in government-controlled schools, or, if they be taught, that the teachers should have full liberty to teach according to their convictions.

To exclude the subjects from the curriculum, even if desirable, would not really solve the difficulty, for every lesson in history or political geography or literature, will carry with it the teacher's point of view, even though he may not intend to communicate it. Freedom for teachers, with all the risks of freedom, seems to be the true alternative. And if there is to be any entry to the schools directly or indirectly, for propaganda, it should be impartially extended to all serious and reputable views. The problem will not be easy to solve, but it cannot be further discussed in this place. What has been said must suffice to indicate its nature.

There remains the press, the platform and the book. The press is perhaps the most powerful agent of propaganda ever created, and it is the more powerful the more it operates by indirection and suggestion. It is one of the most curious and disquieting facts of modern society that this great agency of education should be controlled by men who openly profess that they have no object except to make money and no training in any art but that. For the peace of the world and the security of civilisation no reform would be more important than one which should make the press a profession instead of a branch of commerce, and its editors men of knowledge, science and humanity, with a sense of responsibility for the consequences of their teaching. There are still a few such in England, but the succession of them seems to be in grave peril. Yet among the able young men constantly being recruited for the press there must be some with the capacity to be apostles. One of these perhaps will arise to reform the press as once the Friars reformed the church.

The platform is open to all parties and all causes. It must always be a potent source of education, good or bad. And in this place we need not speak further of it. But of the book a few words must be said. It is already, and may become still more, a powerful instrument of popular education. But, to be so, it must be cheap, and it must be deliberately written for and distributed to the thinking members of the working class. What a large demand there is among these for serious literature is becoming daily more and more evident by actual experiment. It is that demand that workers for peace must set themselves to satisfy. They must rewrite the history and politics of the past and the present in the light of the international ideal. They must destroy the romantic illusions, and insist upon the hard plain facts. They must return again and again, from every angle of approach, to the fundamental problem of war and peace. They must treat war as a problem not an axiom, a catastrophe not a glory, a disease to diagnose not an achievement to idealise. A generation of hard and sober work of this kind might conceivably revolutionise international policy. For it is only by convincing the reason of men that it is possible to impart a steady direction to their action. The way is laborious and difficult. But there is no other.

WAR: ITS NATURE, CAUSE AND CURE

Preface

If an author could choose his audience, I would choose that the following pages should be read by men, and especially young men, who have served in the Army and Navy. To those who already see and feel the menace of modern war, and understand its causes, I have nothing new to say. To militarists, who neither see nor feel, it is idle to speak. But the country is full of young men who are open to the truth, if they had the leisure, the opportunity and the desire to seek it. And to them, in the hope that this book may fall into their hands, I am writing this word of preface. Some of them, perhaps many of them, will have found in war something which they prize and prize rightly. The following passages give some expression to it. A young officer writes to me in a private letter:

"I should not stress too much the horror of war to those who actually took part in it. I know my experiences were with an exceptionally united and successful body of men, and that to many the war was plain hell. But there was, to many of us, very much on the other side. Nor was this a joy in the actual fighting, nor a fascination with tawdry romance. There were greater things. You may say we were spiritually drugged and pathetically deluded. But never before or since have we found them. There was an exaltation, in those days of comradeship and dedication, that would have come to few in other ways. And so, to those of us who have ridden with Don Quixote and Rupert Brooke on either hand, the Line is sacred ground, for there we saw the vision splendid."

The other passage is from an unpublished diary and reads as follows:

"I had in this company a sense of union, of identity, of complete at-oneness and a strength of pure affection which I have never felt for anyone else. Really, I loved without mawkishness or sentimentality and untouched by any feeling of sex or inspiration of an ulterior motive. It seemed a natural love welling up from the heart, because it must, like the love that is supposed to exist between a mother and son, and a sister and brother. It was a spontaneous emotion, an active state unconnected with personal attributes but existing between us because I was I and they were they. It was a personal devotion ideally expressed by 'greater love hath no man than this, that he lay down his life for another.' I think that is one of the good points of war, that it makes you true to others and go outside yourself where he who stands alone is lost. I suppose that is as good for character as the Army is bad. The form has spoilt the spirit, like the difference between Christ's word and what the Churches have made out of it."

I leave these words without comment. They are the record of genuine experience which it is no part of my case to belittle or deny. But the writers, I know, would not suppose that such experiences justify war. They are only something to be set against its evils. What those evils are, and will be, I have tried to set forth here. And also, which may weigh more with some minds, I have shown what the causes of war really are. It is, to my mind, no exaggeration, but a plain truth, that war and civilisation henceforth are incompatible. I would myself go further. I think that the very existence of mankind is incompatible with that further development of methods of destruction on which science is actually engaged. Yet I see little evidence that this truth is grasped by most men or women. No subject is more unpopular, to think or talk about, than war. And the soldiers and diplomats, while their peoples attend to other things, are renewing the whole apparatus of policy which led to the last and must lead to the next catastrophe. I do not see how this is to be met, except by ordinary men and women giving their minds to the real facts. And among those, one would suppose, the most active should be those who know by experience what modern war is like. I will conclude by a passage from a book I cite more than once in what follows, Mr. C. E. Montague's *Disenchantment*:

"There is only one thing for it. There must still be five or six million ex-soldiers. They are the most determined peace-party that ever existed in Britain. Let them clap the only darbies they have – the Covenant of the League of Nations – on to the wrists of all future poets, romancers and sages. We must beware in good time of those boys and elderly fiery men piping in Thessaly."

1

My theme may be put in a sentence: If mankind does not end war, war will end mankind. This has not been true in the past. But it is true in the present. For the present has produced something new. It has produced science. And if science is the principal hope of mankind, it is also the principal menace. For it can destroy as easily as it can create; and all that it creates is useless, if it creates only to destroy. But destruction is what war means; and all its other meanings are made meaningless by this.

Let me illustrate. On this day, March 22, 1922, I read in my newspaper a discussion in the House of Commons on the Aircraft Force. A member (says the account) "drew attention to the probable horrors of the next war. Vast fleets of aeroplanes would come over our towns with bombs of 4,000 or 5,000 pounds containing high explosives, poison gas, and probably cholera germs, and the women and children in those towns would suffer as much as the men engaged in actual warfare." Or take another statement, by Major-General Seeley, ex-Minister of War: "Chemical knowledge was now so far advanced that, with very little trouble and at very moderate cost, a hundred thousand people could be blotted out by lethal gas during an air raid. A great deal of nonsense had been spoken about wonderful discoveries. The truth was that the manufacture of the most deadly gases was easy and inexpensive. It was simple and horrible. The choice was really between disarmament and extermination."

Take another testimony by Thomas Edison: "There exists no means of preventing a flotilla of aeroplanes from flying over London tomorrow and spreading a gas that would poison its millions in three hours. One day science will invent a machine so terrible in its possibilities, so absolutely terrifying that man himself will be appalled and renounce war for ever."

Mr. Edison's science is probably better than his knowledge of human nature. The whole question is, whether that terrible and stupid animal, man, can in fact be frightened off war by the proof that it means his destruction in this bestial way. Perhaps he cannot. But in any case the facts are clear and indisputable.

In all the principal countries of the world, after the "war to end war," men of science are busy investigating methods of destroying by war men, women, children, factories, cities, countries, continents. In part they know how to do it already, in part they are perfecting their weapons; and there is no limit to their powers. This was not true in the past, but it is true in the present, and it will be truer in the future. There is the new fact, that puts out of date all the ordinary discussion of war. War now means extermination, not of soldiers only, but of civilians and of civilisation.

2

But "No," someone perhaps will say, "we will not go so far. We will regulate war so that it shall be waged in the old gentlemanly way. Then we can have war without universal destruction."

But war was regulated before the last war, and the regulation made no difference. Every weapon that could be used for destruction was used. "That was the Germans' fault!" Well, if you like, it was. But we imitated them. We made poison gas, and made it better than they. We made liquid fire, and made it better than they. We made air raids, and made them better than they. And if we did not use the submarine to sink merchant ships, that was only because we could deal with them as easily without. Did not one of our most popular heroes, Lord Fisher, write to the German Admiral Tirpitz: "I don't blame you for the submarine business. I would have done the same myself, only our idiots in England wouldn't believe it when I told 'em"?

It is waste of time to argue about who began this scientific savagery. There has not been, and there will not be, any impartial inquiry. It is enough for us to know that someone will always begin it. And if you choose to believe that that someone will always be not the English, but their enemies, that belief does not alter the argument. Someone will do it, and then, by way of "reprisals," the others will imitate them. For "reprisals" mean doing what you think wrong on the plea that someone else did it first.

Did you notice, the other day, what happened at Washington? The Powers were discussing the use of the submarine in war. The British, to whom imports by sea are more important than they are to any other nation, who therefore fear the submarine more than any other nation, and who also expect always to command the sea, and thus to be able to cut off an enemy's trade without recourse to the submarine – the British, for those reasons, proposed the abolition of the submarine. What did the French reply? That the submarine is a weapon of "defence," not of "offence," and that they proposed to build an enormous fleet of them. The British then produced an article, written by a French Naval Officer, defending all that the Germans did with the submarine in war. The French thereupon repudiated the article, and a rule was solemnly drawn up prohibiting the use of submarines as commerce destroyers. Do you believe that rule will be kept? If so, you are credulous.

Similarly, a rule was adopted at Washington prohibiting the use of poison gas. Do you believe that rule will be kept? It would be interesting to know which of the nations who signed it – the Americans, the British, the French, the Italians, the Japanese – have, since, shut down their establishments for manufacturing poison gas. Have the English? Would you feel happy if they had? Probably not. Probably you think we ought to be "prepared" in case the other fellow breaks the rule. And so does everybody think. But I will go further. Suppose we were losing a war, and thought we could win it by breaking one of these rules. Would you stand for our losing the war rather than making the breach? And if you would, would the Press? Would the Music Halls? Would the War Office? Would the Admiralty? Would Parliament? You know very well, or, if you do not, you ought to know, that every nation considers everything right which may secure it from defeat. I do not know whether those who sign such conventions as were drawn up at Washington really believe they will be observed. I should be surprised if they did. But if they do, then they are not fit to take in hand the policy of nations. For they are relying on a broken reed. No rules to restrain the conduct of war will ever be observed if victory seems to depend upon the breach of them.

In truth, the character of the next war must be judged not from what governments say, but from what they do. Watch their actual experimental work. Watch their constructive work. And be sure that while war exists it will always be as destructive as it can be. For war is not now what once it was in Italy – a game of professionals, in which both sides agree that it is cheaper not to kill the combatants. We fight now to kill, and to kill by every means.

This is so much a matter of course that it is never even disputed, except when somebody remembers that the Public must be deceived. Thus, to return to the debate to which I have referred, the member who called attention to the menace involved by future war, also urged the necessity of defence. And what was his proposal? That we should build a stronger Air Force than the expected enemy (that enemy being, by the bye, that very France which for four and a half years has been our brother-in-arms). "Our Air Force," he said, "was ludicrously weak, France was spending four times as much money on the Air Service as we were." And observe, please, the moral of this. We must be stronger than France; but also, and equally (say the French), France must be stronger than we. Thus, every increase on the one side must be met by a greater increase on the other. And so it is with every arm, and with every nation. Preparing for war means that every nation must continually spend more and more income on making more and more destructive armaments. It means that armies become bigger, guns more powerful, gas more poisonous, germs more potent, and whatever else may be in the heads of these patient men of science more destructive, until the moment comes when all this preparation explodes into action, And then? Then, I submit to you, without any belief that I am exaggerating, then – the end of civilised man.

Every day you, whom I am addressing, go about your work. You marry yourself, or you marry your son or your daughter. You plan for the future. You look forward to life, for yourself, for your children, for your country. The play, the music hall, the concert occupy and amuse you. You read books. You ride in motor-cars. You travel. You hope and aspire. And all this time, side by side with you, in this laboratory, at that harbour, in those barracks, accompanied by cheerful music, wooed by patriotic songs, the agents of destruction are at work. They are people, no doubt, much like others. But their work is to destroy all that those others are building up; to make mockery of all their purposes and hopes; to kill, with incredible tortures, incredible numbers of men. This they are doing as a matter of course, as a patriotic duty. Surely there is something very strange about this! Is a nation, after all, nothing but a crowd of homicidal lunatics?

3

It is worth while to pause for a moment at that question. Perhaps the answer is "Yes." Perhaps, really, men exist to destroy, not to build. I know young men who say so, or who almost say so. And if it be so, the fact cannot be altered by an odd person, like myself, who happens not to be homicidal. I cannot answer my own question one way or the other. But I can at least ask it. And choosing to suppose (absurdly no doubt), that I have before me the men of whom I want to ask it, I will ask it of them one by one.

You, I will suppose, are a sailor. You belong to the Navy that boasts a tradition finer and cleaner than that of any other service. Well, what were you doing in the Great War? One gallant action was fought, so far as I remember. One gallant landing attack was made. There may have been others. You may have been present. You may be, legitimately enough, proud of the fact. But this was not a war, as other wars have been, of naval battles. What then were you really doing, most of the time? Maintaining the blockade, by which, we are sometimes told, the war was won. Well, what was the blockade? An attempt to starve to death the population of Germany, and, in particular (for, of course, the burden would fall first on them), the old men, and women, and little children. Believe me, you were fairly successful in that.

I have been in Germany since the war. I have been at the hospitals, I have seen the crowds of rickety children produced by our blockade. The number of those who died of hunger, or of the diseases caused by hunger, is estimated at hundreds of thousands. That is what you were doing during the war with Germany. Then, when that war was over, you did the same thing to Russia, to our late Ally, to the people who had perished by millions to gain our victory. Russians, too, you starved, so far as you could. Even medical stores you kept out, so that operations by the knife had to be performed without chloroform. That is what your proud service was really doing. Do you like it? Do you approve it? Is it what you want to give your life to? Yet, in every future war, that, more than anything else, will be what a navy will be doing. I am not reproaching you. I am asking you the question. It seems to me that you ought to answer it. And upon your answer, and that of thousands like you, will depend in part the future of mankind. You may, of course – you probably will – choose not to reply, and not to consider. But what you cannot choose is, that your acts shall not produce their consequences.

I turn next to the airmen. Of you, too, it is said that you maintain the tradition of chivalry in war. I daresay you do. You have courage, as almost all men have. You risk your lives, as all soldiers do, and also all doctors and all miners. You bear no malice to your enemy. You drop wreaths on his grave. Yes, all that, and much more, no doubt, of which I do not know. But also, and as your main work, the thing for which you exist, you drop bombs not only on troops but on cities. You were perhaps yourself one of those who dropped them on a circus of little children at Karlsruhe. That was not your object? Very likely. But what has that to do with it? It was your work, and it always will be, and always must be, your work. For you cannot, and will not, pick and choose where your bombs will fall. As I read these words. I come across a little controversy about the action of our Air Force among primitive people. A Flight-Lieutenant writes correcting a statement that the population of a certain village had been destroyed by bombs. The population, he says (no doubt with truth), were first removed. And then he adds: "It is not the custom of the Royal Air Force to murder women and children, or even inflict casualties upon natives, *unless absolutely necessary.*" The italics are mine, and the words italicised contain the gist of the matter. It will not always be possible to remove the inhabitants, even though it be desired, any more than the inhabitants of Amritsar were removed before General Dyer shot into them. Our Flight-Lieutenant, I suspect, would not profess that it was his duty to refrain from bombing unless the inhabitants had been removed. Whatever the intention, and whatever the feelings of the Royal Air-Force, that Force is, in fact, a women-and-children-bombing Force, and cannot help being so.

But, leaving aside this question about "policing," what about the next great war? Everyone knows, and everyone admits, that it will be fought largely in the air, and that the first objective will be the capital cities of the enemy countries. Our Flight-Lieutenant, if he should live to see that day, will be sent to bomb Berlin, or Paris, or Petrograd, or New York, according to the direction which politicians, uncontrolled and unnoticed by him, may have given to our policy. Or again, he will be bombing food-ships in order to starve the whole civil population of the enemy country. Plans for this performance are being worked out elaborately in America. I read today of "a fast-cruising sea ship which will carry a super-giant airship, which will contain a swarm of aeroplanes which can be rapidly put together in the air and started on a mission of destruction. Not only will it be possible to enforce an air blockade at the other side of the world, if necessary, but by employing what is to be called this new 'sea-airplane' on an extensive scale, it would be possible to keep on bombing and harrying, night as well as day, food-ships bringing vital cargoes to any country which was the object of this insidious and terrible form of air attrition." And so on. Now please do not ride off on idle speculations as to whether, as yet, this particular thing is possible. You know very well that, if it is not, it will be. You know that there is no limit to the powers of destruction. The point I want you to attend to is different. During the late war, all the floodgates of rhetoric were opened to condemn the German submarine warfare, because it destroyed merchant ships without warning. Now, in the country which went to war because of that "crime," the experts are working out the means of destroying merchant-ships from the air, without warning or possibility of defence. Well? What about all these moral transports? They were mere talk, expressing anger at an enemy country. Every country engaged in the next war will do things much worse than that, and do it with a clear conscience – if conscience be a word to use in connexion with war. And you? Are you going to do that too? You are, of course, if you are told to. But what do you think of the thing called war that puts you on that kind of job? Are you going to wait passively till you are called upon so to act? Or are you going to join those who intend to stop war? Which is it to be? The question has been asked. The responsibility henceforth is yours. Which is it to be?

And you next, the artilleryman. Perhaps, by the next war your occupation may be gone – I do not know. But, supposing it is not, what do you think of it? Your shells fall a mile or two away. You do not see what happens when they fall. You do not see the limbs blown to pieces. You do not hear the cries and groans. You are cheerful when you hit your mark and depressed when you do not. I know. I have talked to you, and have found you a sensitive, humane man. And, you said, you did not at all mind what you did. No! But was your not minding a result of your not seeing and, therefore, not feeling? I do not know. Once more I ask the question. Have you the right to evade it ?

And you, the infantryman, you on whom fell the main brunt of the war. As you crouched in your lousy trenches, as you went over the top, as you trampled on the faces of wounded men, as you tossed bombs into dug-outs, as you bayoneted men who were stretching hands of surrender, did you really like doing it? Do you want to return to doing it? Do you feel that life would be unbearably flat if there were no chance of your doing it? Perhaps you will say, yes. And if you do, then, of course, you will try to maintain war, and to oppose those who wish to abolish it. All I am asking for is candour. And does not one man owe candour to another, or at least to himself?

4

Among those with whom I mainly associate, it is often assumed that nobody wants war. It is because I believe that assumption to be untrue that I am putting these questions. I believe that many men like war, or think they do, even as war has now become. Do you want evidence? Take the following stories from one of the few English books about the war which are both sincere and well written: Mr. Montague's *Disenchantment*. Mr. Montague went through the war and knows what he is talking about. He is also a trained writer, knowing what words mean. Here are two of his stories:

" 'I fancy our fellows are not taking many prisoners this morning,' a Corps Commandant would say with a complacent grin, on the evening after a battle." Please observe the "complacent grin."

"A certain General told with enthusiasm an anecdote of a captured trench in which some of our men had been killing off German appellants for quarter. Another German appearing and putting his hands up, one of our men – so the story went – called out: 'Ere, there's 'Arry. 'E ain't 'ad one yet.'" The General may have been "kidded" about the fact, as the author remarks. But that makes no difference to his state of mind. He enjoyed the thought of the thing he was describing. How many more enjoyed it among the innumerable inarticulate

I do not know. But I hardly dare think they were few.

To soldiers, need I dwell on this point further? Yes, I believe I must. For they, very likely, are unwilling to look in the direction in which I am pointing. Here are some facts given in a letter to the *Nation*, signed St. John Ervine. Take first, an extract from a British military manual issued by the General Staff. It is headed *The Offensive Spirit*, and runs thus: "All ranks must be taught that their aim and object is to come to close quarters with the enemy as quickly as possible so as to be able to use the bayonet. This must become a second nature." On another page the manual says: "Bayonet fighting produces lust for blood," and urges the platoon commander to increase his own efficiency and thus gain the confidence of his men by "being bloodthirsty and for ever thinking how to kill the enemy and helping his men to do so." Where is the romance, the heroism, the chivalry of war in this book written by men who know what war is for the men who are waging it, not for historians, writers, and enthusiastic women? Let me go on. This is the kind of conversation that really occurred, in the actual experience of this soldier:

" 'If it was permissible to blow a man's body to pieces with a "five-nine," why was it reprehensible to poison him with mustard-gas? If it was permissible to kill him when he was un-wounded, why was it not permissible to kill him after he was wounded? If he were not killed by us, we had to employ stretcher-bearers and doctors and nurses and attendants to take care of him and thus deprive our own men of a certain amount of care. Moreover, we had to feed him! ...' Similarly, with prisoners. 'What was the sense of taking prisoners when they could be more conveniently dealt with by getting them all into a corner and turning a Lewis gun on to them? There would be less food for our own side if we had to feed prisoners! The great capture of Italians at Caporetto must have depleted the Germans' commissariat terribly! ...' So ran the arguments of the logicians, reinforced with the indisputable argument that many prisoners and wounded men had been known to kill those who had spared their lives.

"When one answered these arguments by saying that ruthlessness provoked ruthlessness, the retort was 'War is war!' When one carried the logical argument a little further than was customary, and suggested that since nurses and doctors and Red Cross officials were engaged in restoring wounded men to a condition in which they could return to the fighting line, it would be quite right and proper to make a particular point of killing them, the logicians among us held that the argument was sound. All hospitals ought especially to be bombarded. The Red Cross should be treated as a good mark for gunners! Why should we not follow the example of the Red Indians, who were very careful to kill the babies of a defeated tribe so that they should not grow up and possibly seek revenge? The logicians said that it might come to that some day, little realizing that they spoke prophetically! An enemy could be exterminated, I said, as certain birds and animals had been exterminated, by sparing the males and killing the females. There were some extreme logicians who considered that this was a possible development of warfare. 'Women get very near the front line now,' they said. 'They'll get *into* the front line in the next war! ...' One had to be logical. War was war. The object of the soldier is to destroy his enemy! ..."[17]

I don't know, of course, what the enthusiastic soldier is going to say about this. For myself I have only to say that this is what war really is, when all the glamour has been wiped off, like the tinsel it is. And I submit that the only moral is contained in the words in which my author concludes his letter:

"If war is to persist among men, then the militarists are in the right, and only those nations can hope to survive which have made themselves exceedingly bloodthirsty and have achieved a high efficiency in killing; but if civilization in the sense of cultured institutions is to survive, then we must somehow eliminate the soldier from society. We cannot have soldiers and not have wars, for the soldier with his aspirations is the centre of infection. What is the use of possessing a highly organized and skilful army, the efficient militarist will demand, if it is never tested on the field? And so, for the gratification of professional pride, we shall find ourselves involved again in a devastating conflict. 'And so to the end of history,' as Caesar says in Mr. Shaw's play, 'murder shall breed murder, always in the name of right and honour and peace, until the gods are tired of blood and create a race that can understand.' "

5

The questions I have put, so far, are to combatants, who at least have known what war is; to whom, therefore, one can only say: "Well, if you do like it, you do," and leave them there. But the non-combatants? They do not know, they do not want to know, and they have the least chance of knowing, unless they have a leisure, a detachment, and a desire for truth which is rare. Part of the business of war is to prevent those at home from knowing what this thing is really like which every agency of publicity is urging them to support. I remember hearing of a young soldier who, coming home on leave, went to a cinema that purported to represent the war. He came out heaving a sigh of relief. "Thank God," he said, "It isn't a bit like the real thing. If they saw the real thing, people might want to make peace." We can read now, if we have time and endurance, in books written by soldiers, some true accounts of what the war was like. But there was little enough of that published during the war, and what little there was, was little read. Instead, day after day, was stretched, between the public and the truth, the immense curtain of the Press, as irrelevant to what went on behind it, as is the curtain of any theatre. There were correspondents at the front who knew, and some who could feel. Some of these have written since. But how much could they write at the time? Those at the front suffered and did things insufferable and undoable. But at least they knew. Those at home dealt in words and pictures. And what words! And what pictures! "Tommy" always cheerful. Nurses always gay. Jokes. Concerts. Almost, one might think, a perpetual picnic. The real thing was covered up by the word "casualties." Of these, so many hundreds, so many thousands, so many millions. That was all. Casualties! For most of them agony or death to a soldier at the front. For most of them, long-drawn grief to somebody at home. But all that was left unrecorded. The Press was a huge conspiracy of omission; and, especially, omission of any good thing that was done by the enemy. Says Mr. Montague – who ought to know – "A war correspondent who mentioned some chivalrous act that a German had done to an Englishman during an action, received a rebuking wire from his employer – 'Don't want to hear about any good Germans.'" What a flash suddenly into the pit! Germans, all Germans, every individual German officer, soldier, civilian, ceased, in the Press-mirror, to be human; while every Englishman, Frenchman, Italian, American, became a hero. Here is another example taken at random, for volumes could be filled with this sordid story. Here is the actual growth of one of these Press legends:

Kölnische Zeitung.
"When the fall of Antwerp got known the church bells were rung (meaning in Germany)."

The Matin.
"According to the *Kölnische Zeitung*, the clergy of Antwerp were compelled to ring the church bells when the fortress was taken."

The Times.
"According to what the *Matin* has heard from Cologne, the Belgian priests who refused to ring the church bells when Antwerp was taken have been driven away from their places."

The Corriere della Sera, of Milan.
"According to what *The Times* has heard from Cologne via Paris the unfortunate Belgian priests who refused to ring the church bells when Antwerp was taken have been sentenced to hard labour."

The Matin.
"According to information to *The Corriere della Sera* from Cologne via London, it is confirmed that the barbaric conquerors of Antwerp punished the unfortunate Belgian priests for their heroic refusal to ring the church bells by hanging them as living clappers to the bells with their heads down." [18]

Here is another example, which, at any rate, is humorous:[19]

Extract from the Italian newspaper, *Popolo d'Italia*. Editor, Signor Musolini. Written before Rumania's Declaration of War:	Extract from the same paper, written after Rumania's Declaration of War:
"People must at last cease from describing the Rumanians as our sister nation. They are not Romans at all, however much they adorn themselves with this noble appellation. They are an intermixture between the barbarous Aborigines, who were subjugated by the Romans, and Slavs, Chazars, Avars, Tartars, Mongols, Huns, and Turks, and so one can easily imagine what a gang of rascals has sprung from such an origin. The Rumanian is to-day still a barbarian, and an individual of very inferior worth who, amid	"The Rumanians have now proved in the most striking manner that they are worthy sons of the ancient Romans, from whom they, like ourselves, are descended. They are thus our nearest brethren, who now, with that courage and determination, which are their special qualities, are taking part in the fight of the Latin and Slav races against the German race – in other words, in the battle for freedom, civlisation, and right against Prussian tyranny, domineering, barbarism, and self-seeking. Just as in 1877 the Rumanians showed what

the universal ridicule of the French, apes the Parisian. He is glad enough to fish in muddy waters where none of those perils exist which he seeks to avoid as much as possible, as he has already shown in 1913."

they could achieve by the side of our brave Russian Allies against Turkish barbarism so will they now also with the same Allies, in the face of Austro-Hungarian barbarism and un-civilisation, throw their sharp sword into the scales and weigh them down. Nothing else indeed could be expected from a people which has the honour of belonging to that Latin race which once ruled the world."

This is the kind of stuff that was served out to the people at home, and the people at home liked it, swallowed it, digested it. Horrible as the war was at the front, behind the front it was base. And the rays of that baseness were caught up and concentrated, by the glass of the Press, into that fire of hell that still burns in men's minds.

It would be as idle to complain of this as it would be foolish to be surprised at it. Force and fraud are two sides of one medal, and where the, one is, there will the other be. The Press is the obverse of the gun – the one kills the body, the other the soul. I dwell on the point for a moment only that I may make plain how hard it is to deal with war. For the truth of it is covered up in lies. And the boys now crowding from school into our universities know so little about what was going on, but four years ago, that they are only sorry they could not take part in it, and hopeful of better luck next time. If it has always been hard for men to learn by experience, it is harder ten-fold now, when experience is deliberately camouflaged. Thus, on every hoarding one passes the picture of smiling men, well fed, well dressed, bent, it would seem, on cricket, football and love. "This," say the authorities, "is what war is. Come and join the army." And their notices, I suspect, mean more to young men of nineteen than all the five years of real war.

I do not know how the lie is to be met, except by the truth. But the lie is organised, and the truth is not. And to expect the truth to be organised is to expect too much. For the lie is friendly, sociable, comfortable, and easy, but the truth is ungrateful and austere. That is why journalism prefers the lie; and journalists, whatever their private preferences, can but and do but submit. The teaching of mankind now is done not by any Church; it is done by a small set of newspaper proprietors who have no object except to make money. But it is easier to make money by lies than by the truth. Truth has only one power: it can kindle souls. But, after all, a soul is a greater force than a crowd. These words are written to you, the individual reader. If they strike a light in you, that light will shine, and shining, perhaps, may yet help to save mankind.

6

And now, a word to the men of science, and especially to the chemists. Did it ever strike you that it is your discoveries and your work that has made it possible for war to destroy mankind? I do not say that as a reason against your science. But may it not be a fact relevant to your attitude to war, and therefore to politics? For instance, the other day the British Government asked for chemists to investigate the uses and preparation of poison gas. They had no difficulty, so far as I know, in getting them; and I remember only one protest from a Professor of Chemistry. Those of you who approve of this work, what exactly is your attitude? Do you say: "We have nothing to do with the uses to which our science is put. We are the tools. Politicians are the workmen"? If so, is that an attitude worthy of science? Or do you add: "We are patriots. We owe our services to our Government"? That might be a sufficient answer. But then, something else follows. Governments, and the conduct of Governments, depend upon the electorate, and the electorate depends, in the last resort, upon its leaders. Men of science are commonly also politicians, in some sense. Well, are you enlightened politicians or not? Have you, as citizens, if not as chemists, considered the problem of war? And on which side have you ranged yourselves? I have no wish to be offensive to anyone.

The business is far too serious for that. But hitherto I have found no evidence that men of science are better politicians than other men. By "better," I mean, both better informed and better minded. Specialism is a dangerous thing, when specialists have power but not insight. But insight means a knowledge and a discipline about human society, which is something quite different from knowledge and discipline about some department of nature. I saw, during the war, utterances of scientific men which made me rub my eyes; so passionate were they, so ignorant and so confident, on matters lying altogether outside the speciality of the writer. It was as though these men were not aware that society too is a matter for study, and, above all, for disinterested study. But if a Professor takes his politics from *The Times* or the *Morning Post*, and if that Professor has in his head (as he may have) an idea that can annihilate a nation, what man can be more dangerous than he? I would like to know – I don't know, of course – how many chemists ever think about the relation of their science to human life and human death. If they thought hard enough, their thought, perhaps, would result in a different kind of action. I can imagine, for instance, that this sort of thing might occur: that the chemists and the physicists, and whatever other group of men of science might be concerned, might get together from all countries and announce to all Governments that they, for their part, did not propose to communicate to Governments anything which would be useful in war; that they refused their services for such purposes; and that, if war was to continue to be waged, it must be waged without their help. Would not such a demonstration be likely to have a great effect upon opinion? You will say it is chimerical. Well, but if so, why? Is it chimerical because it could not be done? Or because it is undesirable that it should be done? And if undesirable, why so? Because you are patriots? And patriots in that ordinary sense, in which patriotism works straight for the destruction of mankind? And so works because, although it may be disinterested, it neither knows nor thinks? If so, I dare to say that you, of all men, have no right to be patriotic, in that sense. You have too much power in your hands. But if you were to know, all of you, and think, about the problem of war, then what I have suggested might cease to be chimerical, and become mere commonsense. At any rate, the point I am making is so clear that it should hardly be necessary to make it. It is no longer safe for science to put itself, as a mere blind tool, into the hands of such Governments as in fact we get, and such soldiers as we must always have, so long as there are soldiers at all. There is a fight to the death now going on, not between nation and nation, but between those whose policy must destroy, and those whose policy might save mankind. Of that conflict, science is the very centre.

It is the instrument both of salvation and of destruction. Is it going to remain a mere instrument, passive and indifferent to the issue? Or is it coming out with all its weight, all its prestige, all its intelligence, on the side of those who mean to end war?

7

Among those who mean to end war should be, one would suppose, first and above all, the students of human society. But are they? During the war a distinguished historian sent me a pamphlet in which he argued that war was not only inevitable but desirable. So far from being at the end of it, we were at the beginning. World wars on a colossal scale were just being ushered in. And the attempt to stop that happening was not only foolish, it was wicked. For upon war depended all the virtues of men. In all this there was no argument which could satisfy a child who had any sense of science. The alleged necessity was the weakest of inductions from our imperfect knowledge of the past. The alleged virtues were not demonstrated. The effect of war on the physical character of the population was not even touched upon. Everything necessary to a serious handling of the issue was omitted. Instead of science, we were given an apocalyptic vision of an appalling future, and invited to say that it was very good. And this was only one specimen of the kind of stuff too often turned out by historians. But, of recent years, the tendency has been not so much to melodramatic generalisation, as to what purports to be a bare record of facts. That at any rate, if honestly done, would not do harm, and if it came into the hands of men of political or moral genius might perhaps do good. But, in fact, it is very hard for most historians to do it honestly, so subtle, unconscious, and all-pervading is the patriotic bias. Those who only read the historians of one country may be unaware of this. But turn from a British to a French or a German account of the same series of events, especially in recent history, and you will become aware of it with a shock. History, in any sense in which it can help us, is the history of mankind. But British, French, or German history, written from the British, French, or German standpoint, is often all the more misleading in so far as it pretends (and it may pretend honestly) to impartiality. What we want is the history of Man, written from the standpoint of Man. Perhaps, by degrees, we shall get it. Mr. Wells has made, recently, a gallant beginning. But we shall not get that kind of history until we regard that point of view as right and desirable. And when we do that, we shall have done much to get rid of war. Meantime, war-men must be, and are, the enemies of true and the friends of false history.

But if it is so hard for historians, even in normal times, to escape the patriotic bias, in war time it seems to be impossible. For it becomes, then, a patriotic duty to view the facts that led up to the war from the point of view of one's own country. And the historian is either silent, while the storm lasts, or he joins the cry with the rest. The history written, during the war, about the origins of the war, was, for the most part, not less lamentable than the journalism. It was, in fact, journalism masquerading as history. Those who had taken a favourable view of German policy in the past, who had supported her in 1806, or 1814, or 1866, or 1870 suddenly discovered that her whole history, since Wilhelm II, since Bismarck, since Frederick the Great, had been (in contradistinction to that of all other nations) one long tissue of force and fraud. Often, the causes of the war were reduced to the events that occurred during the last month or the last day before hostilities broke out; and those events, so far as they were known, were misinterpreted and misrepresented. Very likely, a great deal of this writing was honest, as far as the beliefs of the writer were concerned. But, scientifically, it was worse than valueless. It merely added one more stream to the torrent of lies and hate that swept away every nation engaged. The patriotic bias is, no doubt, as prevalent among students of the physical sciences as among historians. But in their case it does not vitiate the science itself; whereas, in the case of the historians it turns it into mere charlatanry. History will always be, of all studies, the most doubtful and uncertain, for its very data, for the greater part of its course, are known only in fragments, and can never be reproduced by experiment. History, therefore, at the best can never be a science. But it might at least be a humane study. Instead of which, in the last seven years, it has been a howling of dervishes.

8

War, it is often said by its apologists, is not the greatest of Evils. To me, on the contrary, it appears to be precisely that, if only because, in addition to its own Evil, it includes and brings with it all others. It kills and mutilates millions by the deliberate action of other millions. That is its specific Evil. But also it produces famine, disease, poverty, crime, vice, the degradation of physical type and of moral standards. Look out now on Europe. What do you see? In England are some two millions unemployed, with no near prospect of their finding employment. They are living on doles and becoming thereby, with every month, more and more unfit to live in any other way. Those employed are struggling, desperately and in vain, to maintain a decent standard of wages and life. And these are the men who were promised, in case of victory, a "land fit for heroes." Victory came, through their efforts, and they are ruined by its consequences. Taxes are crushing as never before in the memory of living men, and there is little enough prospect of alleviation. This is the position of one of the victors, and the most fortunate in Europe. Of the rest, France is bankrupt, Italy not much better, Poland perishing of disease, and the newly "liberated" countries distracted between covert civil and hardly covert foreign war. Of the vanquished,

Austria is on the verge of collapse, and its capital city, once a great centre of civilisation, is sinking in slow agony towards extinction. Turkey is massacring Christians on an even larger scale than before the war. Hungary is in the hands of a Camorra of reactionary militarists, governing by *coups d'états*, murder, and torture. Germany struggles under the burden of an admittedly impossible indemnity, always on the verge of a collapse into chaos and Bolshevism. Of Russia it is hard to say whether she is to count as vanquished or victorious. But in either case her people are perishing, by millions, of famine. Meantime, the victorious states, having won the war which was to end war, remain armed on a greater scale even than before that war, when their excuse for arming was the military power of the nation they have now reduced to impotence and servitude. At a time when every resource of every nation is needed merely to carry on life, they are expending on armaments more than they ever expended in peace time before, and arranging already behind the scenes, the new groupings, which are to result in the new catastrophe. If there are greater Evils than these, I should be glad to know what they are. And these Evils are all the result, and solely the result, of war. If we cannot learn the lesson, there is no lesson we can learn. But I see no sign that it has been learnt by the great mass of people, and especially by those who still direct, unchecked by public opinion, the foreign relations of states.

9

Nevertheless, for my purpose I must assume that the lesson has been learnt by those readers who propose to follow me further. And I shall now take up their next serious argument. "War," they may say, "is, we agree, a bad thing; perhaps it is, as you affirm, the worst thing. But it is inevitable." Why so? This notion of inevitability is probably based upon a knowledge that the course of history has always been accompanied by war. But that is a lazy way of looking at the matter. It would be necessary, if we were studying history, to go further, and examine the specific causes of wars at different periods, I have myself made some preliminary attempt to do this, in a previous book.[20] But here and now I am concerned with the present state of the world. And I ask: Why is war now inevitable?

Perhaps the reader – if he be the kind of reader I have in mind – will say something like this: "There are a number of states, all armed and all expecting war, sooner or later. Among these states there is usually a wicked state, the one which intends to fight England. The war thus prompted will come, one day or another. We English, of course, shall not provoke it, but the other fellow will. So we must be ready. Then whizz-bang! He starts. There's a war. We win, since we are English. We impose our terms. There is a lull. And then the same business begins again. The wicked Power, a hundred year's ago, was France. Then it Was Russia. Then it was Germany. Who it will be next, we don't know. Perhaps France again."

That is really the way many people think about war. But they ought to make an addition, which, in fact, they never do make. It is this: It is not only the English who feel in this way. Every other nation is feeling in the same way. In every war, everybody agrees, somebody is the aggressor and somebody on the defence. But also, in every war, and for every nation, the aggressor is one's enemy, and the defender oneself. As soon as that is grasped, the absurdity of the whole position flashes into view. You say, the foreigner is the aggressor. He, with equal conviction, says you are. The truth does not enter into the question. The people concerned do not know the truth, are not in a position to know it, and do not want to know it. For, as soon as war is in the offing, the notion that one's own country may be to blame is repugnant and intolerable to every patriot. Are we to say, then, that war is inevitable because people inevitably misunderstand one another? That is rather thin ground whereon to proceed to the destruction of mankind.

And really, do you think it likely that, in the long history of Europe, it should so happen that the English alone have always been right and just in their wars, and their enemies always wrong? Do you really believe that we have never been influenced by anything but the desire to do right? If that were so, why has the British

Empire continually increased as a result of our wars, while there is no perceptible increase in the prevalence of Right? It would be a very good corrective, for anyone who really believes this nonsense, to read his history for once in a foreign author. He would get a curious view of British policy and morals. I do not say it would necessarily be truer than our own. But it would not be falser. Such a reader would find that, to foreigners, the British are the aggressive nation above all others. He would find them pointing, among other things, to the British Empire, and asking how we got India, Canada, Egypt, a great part of Africa? How we got, and how, for centuries, we held, Ireland? If he would look further at the history of British wars, he would find that we have almost never made a peace without taking someone's territory. If our wars were solely defensive, why did we do that? It is impossible to understand the causes of war until we put ourselves outside this English standpoint. But as soon as we do that, as soon as we look at history as men, not as Englishmen, the truth stares us in the face. It then becomes plain that all states, in all their wars, have always had a double object: on the one hand, to keep what they have got; on the other, to take more.

This, and this only, is the cause of all wars, other than civil wars. For this double reason, of defence-offence, states have armed. But as soon as they are armed, and in proportion as the armaments are formidable, those armaments themselves become an additional and independent cause of war. For they increase the fears which, in the end, precipitate war, even though they may also, for a time, postpone it. For whenever one state makes itself stronger, another state feels menaced. That state increases its forces, and then the first does the same. As the armaments increase, so does the suspicion, the secrecy, the plotting. The possibilities of peaceable adjustment are poisoned at the source; and war becomes really "inevitable," precisely because everyone is fearing it and preparing for it. This truth is illustrated by the history of all states for centuries, but, to a degree unknown before, during the years preceding the late war. It became so palpable at that time, it emerged with such lucidity, that one might have thought that the old fallacy : "If you want peace, prepare for war," would have been finally discredited. Obviously, however, it has not been. Our generals, admirals, politicians still shout it to a bamboozled world with apparent conviction. Yet there are signs of progress. The opposite view is also to be heard from leading men. For example, as I write, I come across the following remarks of Mr. Lloyd George, who has, at any rate, more sense of facts than most statesmen, whatever may be thought of his way of dealing with them. Speaking the other day of that massing of troops on the frontiers of states which marks the end of the war to end war, he remarked: "It is the fears of nations that make conflicts. Russia may be afraid of an attack from Roumania or Poland, and Roumania may be afraid of an attack from Russia. These fears make conflicts, when troops begin to mass and double and increase and march towards each other." The other view – that the security for peace consists in the accumulation of armaments – could never be true until one state' had succeeded in disarming all the rest. Then there might, indeed, be peace. But long before that could happen, mankind would have been destroyed.

The real cause of war, then, in the modern world, and whenever, in history, there have existed independent states armed against one another, is, first, the desire of all states to hold what they have and to take what belongs to others; next, the armaments produced by that situation, which armaments then become themselves a further cause of war. Given that position, and you may say, without exaggeration, that war is inevitable. There remains only the manoeuvring for position. In earlier times, when there was no pretence of democracy, and the feelings of peoples could be ignored, this manoeuvring was directed mainly by considerations of force; and you get, for example, the spring of Frederick of Prussia upon Silesia. But during the nineteenth century, when political conditions have made it necessary to elicit a more active support on the part of peoples, it has become important for states to appear in the position of the attacked, rather than of the attacker. They can then pose as injured innocents. In the late war, it was we and our Allies who were successful in this endeavour. The Austrians and Germans really did, in the last month, precipitate the war. And that fact was sufficient to bring out, on the side of their opponents, the sentiment of patriotism in its full strength.

On the other hand, the fact that the enemy Governments did, in this sense, provoke the war, was not enough to prevent their peoples from waging it for four years and a half. Still, the fact that the immediate blame fell upon the Austrian and German Governments was no doubt a real asset to the enemies allied against them, and in particular induced many states (especially those of America), that might otherwise have remained neutral, to come in on the side of the ultimate victors. It would, however, be childish – and even historians begin to admit it – to go on thinking that the war was caused simply and solely by this action of Germans and Austrians at the last moment. It was caused by the whole situation of the European states for years past.

And unless a real and successful attempt had been made to alter radically both the purposes of Governments and their means of achieving them, the war would have been ultimately precipitated in some other way, even if the crisis of 1914 had been overcome.

10

I propose, immediately, to describe the larger and deeper causes that really produced the Great War. But before doing so I will make a brief digression. For there is another view about the causes of war, with which we are confronted, sometimes by friends of war and sometimes by its enemies. Both alike are impatient of careful analysis of the way in which wars do actually come about. Both prefer to attribute them to some profound property of human nature, rather than to shallow policies of the human mind. And the inference drawn is, that it is idle to consider the political causes of war, for war will happen simply because men are bellicose.

What truth is there in this?

It will be easier for me to deal with the question if I may suppose that one of these ordinary, simple, unreflecting men is reading me. I would then ask him: During the years of peace, are you really fretting, all the time, because you haven't the chance of killing somebody, and of dying yourself? Because you are not showing your courage in this particular way? Because there are passions and instincts in you urging you not merely to fight (perhaps you do fight, and have fought, this or that man at home), but to make war; that is, to be part of a huge machine the object of which is mass-killing?

I hardly think that the question would even be understood by most ordinary Englishmen. I hardly think many Frenchmen even would understand it. Some few men, no doubt, mistrained in literature and philosophy, might understand, and might even say "Yes." But you, the man I suppose myself to be talking with, however restless, however dissatisfied, however ambitious, however self-sacrificing, will you say that, during the years of peace, you were longing for war? That it was your desire for war that caused the explosion of war? Or even, that your sense of the inevitability of war made you hasten its coming, as a man may throw himself before an express train? No. That, I believe, you will agree, is a false account of the facts. Men may be restless and dissatisfied, but they do not say: "Now, let's have a war to get rid of this feeling."

On the other hand, if it were not for certain things in the ordinary man, of course war could not be provoked. Men are passionate, unreflective, capable of anger, of excitement, of illusion. So that, when certain appeals are made, they may be counted on to respond. They do not care about the purposes which move those who control policy. Simply, if they are told "The country is in danger," "We have been insulted," "Someone is trying to take away something we ought to have," "Someone has attacked us," a charge goes off in them and there is an explosion. In that charge are included all sorts of passions; some not ignoble, such as "Now I shall see whether or no I am a coward"; and some ignoble, such as "Now I shall be free to give way to my lusts." It is this magazine of passion coming down to us from animal ancestors, and embellished and decorated by proverbs, phrases, stories, religion, literature, philosophy – it is this that goes off when it is touched.

Yes. But who touches it? For it does not go off of itself. Nor does it, of itself, ache for that peculiar satisfaction that only war can give it. Generations have lived without war, and felt no loss. And also generations have had war, and felt no gain. The leap of relief with which passions and desires, thwarted and tense, jump at war, is but a first movement before war begins. As soon as men are in it, they are in a machine. And then begins the weariness, the disillusionment, the animality, the bestiality, until, cynical and worn out, the survivors survive only to continue a mechanical activity till "victory" is achieved or lost. And then? A burst of relief, followed by years of toil, frustration, self-indulgence, or despair.

Is that, or is it not, a true account of what happens to you, the ordinary man, in war? Once more I can but ask. But you ought to consider and answer. For upon the answer to such questions depends the fate of mankind.

But if I am right, if I am right even in part only, or right essentially though not in detail, then my argument remains right too. Wars are caused, not by these passions of ordinary men, but by the playing upon them by particular men. And this playing upon the passions is the cause of wars, as much as the spark is the cause of the explosion. The process is this: A mass of men, passionate, and whose passions find imperfect vent in the ordinary occupations of civil life; armed forces, waiting to be used; statesmen and journalists with policies; policies involving war; then the drop of the spark, the crisis, the declaration of war, and, simultaneously, the leap of these passions of men into the new vent opened to them. And then, it lies so near to say: "The passions made the war." But they did not. They were only a necessary condition of the war being made. And they might go on existing, for years and centuries, without war, if the other, the real causes, were not brought into existence. What are those causes? In general terms, I have already described them. I will proceed now to indicate them, in more detail, for the case of the late war.

11

With a view to clearness, we will divide the issues into those of the West and those of the East. In the West there were two main facts making for war. The first was the friction between France and Germany, due to the seizure by Germany of Alsace-Lorraine in 1870. The population of Alsace was wholly German, in origin and speech, and that of Lorraine largely so; and both provinces had been stolen by the French, in the past, from the German Empire. Their seizure by Germany might therefore plausibly be said to be a "recovery," not an "annexation," and was so regarded at the time by Germans and by a great part of the British. But the very fact of the friction produced between France and Germany for all those forty years, is proof that it was none the less bad policy. The question of Alsace-Lorraine lay like a shadow across the map of Europe. It was a chronic source of the poisoning of international relations.

Meantime, Germany, after a financial crisis due to the taking of indemnities from France – a crisis, of course, not comparable to that from which Europe has been suffering since the peace, but due to the same cause, the attempt to make the enemy pay for the war – Germany, now united, proceeded to develop by her industry, intelligence and resources, immense manufacturing and trading power. She became the principal rival of Great Britain. Her merchant ships, her agents and her travellers spread over the world, until, about 1900, she said: "I must have a navy." Her reason for this is only too clear, and too good, in the anarchy in which the nations hitherto have lived. If she had no navy, she had nothing to defend her trade in case of war with England or France. And when might not war come? So the Germans, not unnaturally, reasoned, as we should certainly have reasoned in their place. The response from England was equally natural. We tried, first, between 1899 and 1902, to make an alliance with Germany. The principal advocate of this policy was Mr. Chamberlain, but Lord Lansdowne also approved, and so did other leading British statesmen. If these negotiations had succeeded, we should, no doubt, have had a war, because the whole policy of all nations presupposes war. But it would have been war against Russia and France, and on the side of Germany. It was, indeed, precisely the expectation that that would be so, that seems to have made the Germans cold towards our offers. Up to that date, our principal friction had been with France, commonly regarded, and with much reason, as our hereditary enemy. We were nearly at war with her on several occasions, most notably over the Soudan in 1898. But now, failing to come to terms with Germany, we turned to France. This was one of the great revolutions in European diplomacy; revolutions which, however, always leave everything the same, so far as the lives of the peoples are concerned; for they are merely changes in the grouping of Powers, not in the nature of diplomatic relations.

Our agreement with France turned mainly on the two questions of Egypt and Morocco. Egypt is an old story on which we need not dwell. We took it, partly to secure the money of our bond-holders, partly to control the route to India; and France had been quarrelling with us ever since, because she had not accepted our invitation to go in and take it with us. Morocco, though an old question, is one less familiar. For a long time France had been wanting to take it, and for a long time we had stood in her way. Then came our attempt to ally ourselves with Germany, and it was proposed by leading ministers that we should divide Morocco with her; she to have (curiously enough) that port, among others on the Atlantic, about which, ten years later, we nearly made war on her because we thought she wanted to take it. When we made the entente with France we gave her Morocco, in exchange for her leaving us alone in Egypt. But the treaty by which we gave it her was secret. She was to wait her opportunity, and we were not to interfere. The Moroccans, naturally, were not consulted in the matter. They were only "natives," who would one day be useful as conscript soldiers for France, but otherwise deserved no consideration. This agreement with France is interesting as showing, first, that states can settle their disputes without war; but, secondly, that they seldom do so in fact, except when the motive is to act in common against some other state. In this case, the state that England and France were to act against was Germany. And no sooner had we made our Entente with France than we had our first quarrel with the new enemy. It was over this very question of Morocco. Germany's offence was that she desired to keep the trade of that country open to all others (as, by a public treaty dating thirty years back, it was supposed to be). There followed an international Conference, at which the French and the British agreed with the other Powers to maintain the independence and sovereignty of Morocco, while they kept in their pockets their secret treaties dividing it between France and Spain. For a time, after this, France aimed at a joint Franco-German economic exploitation of the country. This, however, was but a temporary device. Finally, in 1911, she made her military expedition. There followed an explosion from Germany, and France and England came within an ace of War with that country. We could not, we said, tolerate that she should seize that port on the Atlantic, which we had offered her ten years before. We were all righteous indignation. Germany gave way, taking what is called "compensation" elsewhere. And the crisis, for the moment, passed, leaving the usual ill feeling behind it.

Meantime, the first Moroccan crisis had raised the whole question of military cooperation between England and France. Mr. Haldane, thereupon, with great energy, skill and success, organised an Expeditionary Force to go, in case of need, to France. At a later date, naval cooperation was also arranged, our fleet leaving the Mediterranean to be guarded by the French, on the understanding that when the war came, we would protect the coasts of France. Thus the Entente had really passed into something not easy to distinguish from an alliance. Sir Edward Grey could, indeed, say with truth in 1914 that, technically. Parliament was free to decide whether we would go to war or not. But in fact, as he said, and as we thought, we were bound "in honour" to support France. These military and naval arrangements had been made without consultation with, and without the knowledge of, the House of Commons, or even of the majority of the Cabinet. We knew of the Entente and approved it. But we did not know of the military and naval engagements, nor yet of the secret treaty about Morocco.

The Entente with France was made by Lord Lansdowne. It was followed, in 1907, by the Entente with Russia, arranged by Sir Edward Grey. Once more it was shown that the long friction between two states could be peaceably adjusted; but, once more, only if the new friendships involved a new enemy. Sir Edward Grey, it is true, did not desire hostility to Germany; he said – and no doubt said truly – that it had always been his desire to bring her into friendly relations with the other Powers. But there is no evidence that, at any time, this was either the intention or the desire of the French or the Russian Government. On the contrary, passage after passage in the despatches shows that that was precisely what they were afraid of. France, or, rather, certain influential people in France, wanted something she could only get by war, the recovery of

Alsace-Lorraine. She might not *make* war for that, but, with that in view, she would contemplate, not without satisfaction, the possibility of war, if it could be shown to have been provoked by Germany, and if there were a sufficient chance of victory. The position of Russia was rather more complicated. There was an intimate relation between the Tsar and the Kaiser, in which the latter dominated the former. And nothing is more curious than to see these two third-rate men, one little more than an imbecile, the other hardly sane, dealing, in private meetings, letters, and telegrams, with the prosperity of nations and the life blood of millions of men. That kind of thing we may, perhaps, hope has gone once for all out of Europe, and that is perhaps the only good thing the war has produced.

Partly owing to this personal relation of the Kaiser and the Tsar, the policy of Russia is somewhat obscure to follow. As a rule, she worked with the Entente, but there were relapses towards Germany which distressed and disturbed Sir Edward Grey. Broadly, however, it may be said that Russian policy was directed against Germany, and directed, definitely and consciously, towards a war. There were, in fact, two objects which Russia could not achieve, or thought she could not, in any other way. One was the control of the Bosphorus and the Dardanelles, the straits which give her an outlet from the Black Sea to the Mediterranean, and which, of course, were then held by Turkey, The control of these straits was an old object of Russian policy although, from time to time, for various reasons, she paused in the active pursuit of it. We ourselves fought one war in the Crimea to thwart that ambition, and nearly fought another in 1877 for the same reason. But the Entente had altered our policy. We were now more afraid of Germany than of Russia; and it would appear that Sir Edward Grey had given assurances to the Russians that they could have the straits at any suitable moment. The French also, no doubt, would have assented, though reluctantly. Presumably, however, Germany – though once Bismarck had said that the question of the straits was not worth the bones of a single Pomeranian grenadier – would now have opposed Russia. For Germany was building the Baghdad railway, and looking forward to a great extension of commercial influence in Turkey. At any rate, Russia thought she could not get the straits without war. We know this definitely, because there has now been published an account of a meeting of the Russian Crown Council in the February of 1914, six months before the Great War, in which a European war was said to be imminent, and arrangements were made for the military steps to be taken by Russia in order that she might secure the straits. So much for the innocent nations of the Entente, seeking nothing by war, and surprised in their peaceable avocations by a predatory Germany!

The second object of Russian policy was supremacy in the Balkan Peninsula. The long horrors, the intricate perplexities, the intrigues and counter-intrigues, the popular passions and the diplomatic manoeuvres, that for so long have made that little piece of ground the plague spot of Europe, we cannot now pause to describe. It will be enough to attend to certain main facts.

The Balkan States, those bellicose hordes of primitive and violent men, had won, by war and diplomacy, their independence of Turkey. But there remained in 1912 the province of Macedonia still misgoverned by Turkey, though inhabited for the most part by people whom the Bulgarians said to be Bulgarians, the Serbs to be Serbs, and the Greeks to be Greeks. Macedonia was "liberated" by the Balkan wars of 1912-13, but no sooner had the Turks been expelled than the Christian allies fell to quarrelling about the spoils. As a result, the greater part of the province was divided between Serbia and Greece, though it would seem that the bulk of the population is really Bulgar.

Meantime, Russia and Austria-Hungary had both, for years past, been watching the situation, intriguing and co-operating with, or antagonising, one another, in order to secure their interests, or what they supposed to be such, in the Peninsula. This is a very long and complicated story, and of interest only to those whose painful task it has been to study the worst passions of men devoted to the foolishest ends. Both states wanted to dominate the Balkan Peninsula, because both wanted to own or control ports on the Adriatic or the Aegean Sea. At the time of which we are speaking, Serbia was the friend of Russia. She had largely increased her territory, as the result of the Balkan wars. And there were, in the Austrian Empire, large numbers of Serbs whom the Serbian State desired to unite with herself, destroying, by the process, the Austro-Hungarian Empire. The sympathies and policy of Russia were all on the side of the Serbs, partly because the view had been propagated, among influential and patriotic Russians, that the Serbs were their "little brothers" – very much as many Englishmen regard Ulstermen as their little, or big, brothers; partly because the Serbs might be expected to be favourable to Russian ambitions in the Balkans, if only because they were hostile to those of Austria. During the Balkan wars, the great Powers had managed to keep out of the war, though only by hook or by crook. But it is worth noting that, just before the peace that ended the Balkan wars, Austria approached Italy to ask her whether she would join her in making war on Serbia. Italy, backed by Germany, refused, and Austria kept quiet. Meantime it was clear that there were these two questions which Russia intended to settle in her own interest: the question of the straits and that of the Balkans; and that she did not believe they could be so settled except by war.

And Germany? The awkwardness and bluster of German diplomacy, the silly, violent talk of her newspapers and reviews, the cult of war as a great and noble thing, the talk about "shining armour," and all the rest of the paraphernalia of romance, was disgusting and disquieting to other states. Germany was certainly a disturbing element in Europe. But, so far as I am aware, no evidence has yet been published which implicates her in any attempt or design to break the peace prior to 1914 – implicates her, I mean, in any special way, apart from that rivalry of all states which is the real cause of war. Crisis after crisis arose, during the ten years preceding the Great War, and in every one of them Germany seems to have tried, as much as any other state, to keep the peace. You can, of course, say – as became the fashion when the Great War broke out – that she had been preparing not only war, but the war, for ten years, forty years, a hundred and fifty years! There is nothing men and historians will not say, and even think, when their passions are excited. But the fact is that all that talk is sheer nonsense. In Bismarck's time, between 1875 and 1890, Germany was the principal bulwark of peace in Europe. And if she became, later, a disturbing element, it was not because she was planning war, more than other states; it was because she now had a policy which, like that of other states, must entail the risk of war. She wanted an extension of her commercial and political power in the East; and that brought her into conflict with England and Russia. She wanted colonial expansion; and that made her seem dangerous to France and to ourselves. These objects, in the anarchy of European policy, constituted a danger of war. But they did not, of themselves, make it "inevitable." For, in fact, by 1914 England and Germany had come to an agreement about the questions most dangerously dividing them. By that year one must conceive the nations full of mutual suspicion, piling up armaments which made that suspicion continually more deadly, but not, at that moment, any of them, determined on war; partly because they were afraid of it; partly because they were all reluctant to make war unless they felt sure of victory, and unless the enemy could clearly be put in the position of the aggressor. Nevertheless, the war was there, waiting. The powder was collected; the little boys were creeping about, in the dark, with lighted matches. It was just a question who would first drop one. And the boy who did drop it was the little primitive, barbarous, aggressive state of Serbia.

On June 28, 1914, the Crown Prince, the heir to the Austrian throne, was assassinated at Serajevo in Bosnia. If we wish to understand the effect of this act, we may take an analogy. Suppose that, some time in 1920, the Prince of Wales had been murdered by Sinn Feiners in Ireland. Suppose, further (for that is necessary to make the parallel complete), that Ireland were not separated from England by St. George's Channel, but were joined to us by a land frontier. Suppose further that the Atlantic were cancelled, and that millions of Irish just over the border, in America, were plotting, along with our own Sinn Feiners, to destroy the British Empire. How should we have felt in that case? How should we have dealt with proposals to submit the dispute to the Hague Court? Can you not imagine the fury of the British press? Can you not hear the dogs and wolves howling? Well, it was much the same in Austria. The Government, supported and egged on by public opinion, determined to punish Serbia, and make her powerless for the future. In this they were supported, through thick and thin, by Germany, and especially by the Kaiser. That romantic and hysterical man was horrified at the murder of a crowned head, and especially of the heir to the old Emperor, for whom he felt attachment and reverence. But there were also political reasons of a more serious kind. In view of the balance of power (that fetish of all statesmen and all historians), and in view also of her connections with Turkey and the East, it was necessary for Germany to maintain the Austrian Empire, and to prevent the route eastward from being cut by Balkan states under Russian domination. Germany therefore said to Austria: "Get rid of the Serbian menace once for all. We will support you if there is trouble with Russia." For they had bluffed Russia in 1908, and they hoped to bluff her again. That was the situation. Rapidity and secrecy were essential. The ultimatum to Serbia was to be presented before the other Powers knew what it was; it was to be of a kind which it would be impossible for Serbia to accept; and it was to be followed immediately by war. On July 23rd, a month after the Serajevo murder, the ultimatum was presented.

What followed has been the subject of more elaborate analysis, more passionate accusations, more tendencious and dishonest exposition, than any series of events in history. But the main facts are now clear. Russia did not, apparently, desire war at that moment, but was determined to fight if Austria proceeded to crush Serbia. As far as any moral question is here concerned, in the superficial sense in which men think of morals, it turns upon the right of Russia to adopt this attitude. The Austrians and Germans said, and say, that the question was one solely between Austria and Serbia; much as, in the parallel I suggested above, we should have said that the question was one solely between England and Ireland; or as we did say, at the time of the Boer War, that it was one solely between England and the Boers, rejecting any proposal of mediation. Russia, on the other hand, regarded it as a Russian question. Why? For reasons of power. She wanted to dominate the Balkans and to prevent Austria Hungary from doing so. But this power-motive, as we have seen, was reinforced by the belated and uncertain doctrine of racial kinship with the Serbs. The exact question, so long as we keep the discussion on those lines, is whether there is a better justification for one empire to maintain itself against disruption, than for another empire to extend and consolidate its power at the cost of the first. On this question, once it is clearly put, an eternal and unprofitable controversy might be waged. But, in fact, so long as power-policies are the motive of all states, Right and Wrong in international affairs has no meaning. It is a mere extra-weight, thrown in by those responsible, to justify positions adopted for other reasons. I leave the matter at that, insisting only, once more, that that is the core of the whole question, for those who still suppose it to be important to think on such lines at all. Statesmen themselves, and soldiers, and sailors, and all who really determine policy, do not in fact so think. They consider, at every crisis, whether it is or is not worth while to have a war, for the sake of power or territory or markets; and they then paint the moral camouflage, so that the situation may look well for their country.

Meantime, to return to our summary account, France, it was well known, would fight on the side of Russia if there were war about the Balkans. That had been made clear in the previous crisis. France, no doubt, was not strictly bound so to act. She could have said that, in such an issue, the *casus belli* contemplated by her treaty with Russia did not arise, and then, no doubt, Russia would not have fought. But in that case Austria and Germany would have gained an access of strength, and France wanted precisely the contrary. The Balkan issue, therefore, was to be the signal for the conflict between France and Germany, if that issue came to war. And this Russia knew. Under such circumstances the attitude of England might be decisive. Sir Edward Grey wanted peace and worked for it. All the attempts made by Germans to show him as plotting for war have broken down. His case was better and more tragic than that. Caught up in the European anarchy he could see no better course than to bind himself closer and closer to France and Russia, with a view to thwarting what seemed the greater peril of Germany. If there were war between France and Germany, he was bound "in honour" to support France, unless France, in some obvious way, "provoked" war, which, under the circumstances, and with her intelligent statesmen, she was not likely to do. Still, though thus entangled with the enemies of Germany, Grey might have hopes of mediating successfully, as he had done, with Germany's support, in 1912-13, during the last Balkan crisis. He certainly now made every effort to do so. And equally certainly these efforts were thwarted, at first, by Germany as well as by Austria. For those states meant to have war, the Serbian war at any rate, and, if Russia and France should intervene, also the war with those countries.

That was the position at first. But then, as the crisis became acute, Germany wavered. She found that she could not rely on the support either of Italy or of Roumania, and that she might have England against her. She reversed her policy and began urging Austria to concessions which might obviate war. But Austria procrastinated till it was too late. For already, as early as July 29th, Russia had mobilised on all fronts, while falsely saying she had not.[21] On discovering this fact, Germany, on July 31st, replied by her ultimatum to Russia and to France. And the war, so long played with and so long postponed, was at last precipitated.

Belgium, of course, did not come into the causation of the war at all. The attack on her was a consequence, not a cause. But it made a great difference to England. For though we were, at any rate, bound, as most people think, to enter the war, and though, in fact, Grey had made it clear that we should fight, whether or no Belgium were invaded, yet there would have been more hesitation in England, and more division of opinion, but for that act of Germany. From that point of view the invasion may be said to have been a godsend to our

Government. And it certainly influenced the attitude of a great number of brave and honest young men, who went into the war as though it were a crusade. What it really was, we have seen, and we see now, daily and hourly.

12

In the last section I have given a general account of the diplomacy which led up to the war. It will be clear from that sketch how far from the truth is the popular idea, for which hundreds of thousands perished, that Britain and her Allies were fighting a crusade for Right, and had themselves no material objects to pursue, similar to those which were sought by the Germans. But this demonstration, based though it be on evidence that cannot be disputed, does not convey the full cynicism of the statesmen of Europe. That can only be arrived at by records of their talk; and those unfortunately are not easily available. It happens, however, that one book has been published which gives detailed accounts of conversations with some of the actors in the great drama. It deals with the attempt made by the Austrian-Emperor Karl, in the year 1917, to make peace through the medium of Prince Sixte of Bourbon, and records, in notes taken at the time, the conversations held. From this book it seems worth while to take a few examples.[22]

We will begin with the question of the left bank of the Rhine. It may be remembered that a treaty had been made in 1917, between France and Russia (kept secret from the other Allies) whereby this district, inhabited solely by Germans, was to be separated from the German Empire and put under the control of France.

The separation was to be called "neutrality"; but one can imagine the kind of neutrality the French would have been likely to permit. This matter is referred to in a conversation between Prince Sixte and the French President, M. Poincaré.

"The Prince said that he himself went even further than the President and held that we ought to neutralise all the left bank of the Rhine. The President smiled as he answered that one could not always say everything that one felt, but that his views and the Prince's were practically the same." [23]

We see from this little episode that the French of 1917 were exactly like the Germans of 1870, only worse. For the sake of their own security they meant to detach from Germany some millions of Germans and put them under French hegemony. The results of course would have been the same as those of the German annexation of Alsace-Lorraine – a continual friction ending, on a favourable opportunity, in war.

We will pass on now to another point equally significant. The negotiations to which we are referring, for peace with Austria in 1917, broke down because of the opposition of Italy. The conduct of that state for years past had been a masterpiece of what one of her statesmen has fondly called "sacred egoism." Italy was a member of the Triple Alliance. But also, for many years, she had been in close touch with the opposite combination, and had so arranged her treaties that on the one hand she could claim assistance from her allies if attacked herself, and even call upon them to support her in an aggressive war against France; but on the other could refuse assistance to them in case of war between Germany and France. Thus situated, Italy announced, from the beginning, that she regarded the Austrians and Germans as the aggressors and therefore did not hold herself bound to assist them. At the same time, she made it plain that her neutrality was to be had for a consideration. The consideration, of course, was territory belonging to Austria, but inhabited by Italians. There followed a long duel between the members of the two alliances for the favour of Italy. Finally, the Entente were held to have made the best offer, and Italy came over to their side against her own allies. She was to be paid out of Austrian territory; and thus arose the difficulty of making the separate peace with Austria. Italy had to be squared, and it was not possible to square her, for Austria would not offer what she wanted. Her claims do not appear to have been popular with her new allies, and the references to her, cited in the conversations of French statesmen, are singularly rude. One might almost suppose that the two nations were not bound together in a wholly disinterested crusade for Right. "Italy's ambition," said M. Paul Cambon, French Ambassador in London, "inspires her to all kinds of mischief." [24] Ambition, and in a state fighting for Right! Can we have heard correctly? Yes, it is indeed so! For in a second interview the same statesman remarked that Italy "had announced again and again that she had come into the war solely to conquer the territories she coveted." [25]

The recalcitrancy of Italy annoyed that lover of the French, Prince Sixte. "Could we not," he asked, "put pressure on her by refusing her coal and shipping?" "No," says M. Cambon sadly, "for that would be tantamount to a declaration of war." [26] Finally, when the war is over – the war for Right against Wrong – Italy, in the opinion of M. Jules Cambon, late French Ambassador in Berlin, will immediately join hands with the representatives of Wrong! "There can be no doubt that in forty-eight hours after peace is signed Italy will be in the arms of Germany." [27]

M. Cambon's brother agrees. "Italy will do nothing for us. She has only one idea, to perfect her preparations for joining in the economic struggle after the war when all the other allies are exhausted." [28] All this was a libel on Italy? Perhaps, and perhaps not. What is Italy? The young men who were dying in their thousands? Of that Italy, who can speak? But the Italy referred to means the statesmen who brought that other Italy into the war. And the France referring to it means the French statesmen, not the French combatants. We are dealing here with the pullers of the strings, not with the dolls pulled, and we are seeing how the pullers of one ally really looked to those of the other.

Let us turn now, still in the same connexion, to Constantinople. Many people who took seriously the alleged objects of the war thought that one thing it might do was to settle, in a sense favourable to peace, the question of Constantinople and the Straits. Whether the assignment of the prize to Russia would have been a satisfactory solution may be doubted. But that solution was adopted in the Secret Treaty of 1915. Then came the Russian revolution, and Russia became, first suspect, then an enemy, to the fighters for Right. For she had a Government which threatened what was, to these propertied men, more important even than Right, the basis of property. The French drew a long breath. They had never wanted the Russians in Constantinople. They preferred a weak Turkey there, as more favourable to French ambition. "Certain people," said M. Jules Cambon, "make ideal allocations of territory to all the nations: Constantinople to Russia, for instance; there we were much too precipitate. That was a great mistake. ... Then the entire Adriatic to Italy. As for ourselves," he adds sadly, "we shall be left as cold as charity." But then a gleam of comfort enters. "There are territories for us too in the Turkish domains."[29] Territories? But we thought we were fighting for Right! Did you? Deluded men! Those of you who have survived know better now.

To return to our theme. Italy being unwilling to forgo her claim on Austrian territory, an attempt was made to square Austria by offering her territory in Germany. The French negotiators suggested Silesia and Bavaria, out of the German spoils; they planned, that is, the complete dismemberment of Germany, by way of reprisals for the seizure by Germany in 1870 of two French provinces, inhabited almost entirely by Germans.

The Austrians replied that, apparently, Silesia and

Bavaria were not as yet French to give. That matter, accordingly, was dropped, and booty in Africa was substituted. "The Prince then suggested that one of the Italian colonies might meet his (the Emperor Karl's) requirements. Tripoli was barred as a too recent acquisition which would yield nothing, and was too close to Italy. There remained Erythraea and Somaliland. The latter in particular had a future before it, and was quite unknown to the great majority of the Italians; he could say confidently that they would not resent its cession; while, from the Austrian point of view, the novel experience of an African dominion could only be pleasant, especially when it was taken in exchange for a crowd of blustering and uncontrollable irredentists. A negro was, in short, better value than an irredentist." [30] Better value! Observe. The negro is a piece of goods to the fighters for Right. You transfer him as you transfer a bale of cotton. It will be "pleasant" to own him. The Germans also wanted to own some negroes. "Oh, the Germans! But *that* meant the domination of the world! But *that* meant exploitation. But *that* – by God, that was wrong! Come, young men, enlist, enlist; fight the war for Right!" And you came. And you fought. And millions of you died. And tens of millions were wounded and crippled. And now you starve.

And Right? And the end of the war? Well, as to that, your shepherds, in their private talk, were less optimistic than yourselves. Let us listen to another conversation: "The period after the war," said Prince Sixte, "would be terrible." And M. Jules Cambon replied: "Yes, after the war we shall begin to regret the war, for we shall find ourselves faced with difficulties the like of which were never seen before." [31] What! Was that all? Not, then, a war to set the world right? But to produce "worse difficulties than ever were known before?" British statesmen agree. "The financial problem was then discussed. Bonar Law summed up thus to Mr. Lloyd George: 'The money shortage will not stop the war, but after the war we shall be crippled. As Prime Minister during the war you have a very hard time, but the man who will be Prime Minister after the war will have a pretty bad time too.'" [32] Mr. Lloyd George assented. But that was not going to affect his conduct. No indeed! "None of the belligerents would be held up by lack of money." They would perhaps get it out of the Germans afterwards? How successful they would be in that, we are seeing and shall yet see. But money, money, what's money? The lack of money only means unemployment; only means poverty; only means despair; only means soldiers walking the streets begging or stealing; only means the end of all social improvement; only means, at worst, the end of European society. What does it matter, when Right is at stake? – Right interpreted as we have seen it interpreted? Take your gruelling, and take it quietly! Haven't you won the war?

13

In the previous sections I have indicated, briefly, but sufficiently for our present purpose, the real causes of the war. It will have been observed that power, markets, and territory were, on all sides, the only motives operative in the minds of the statesmen who were conducting, in the dark, the policies of Europe. Nevertheless, it is also true that it was Austrian and German policy that, in the last month, actually precipitated the war; though the Russian mobilisation, undertaken at the moment it was solemnly denied, was also an important contributory cause. The reader may therefore think that, after all, all the Right was on one side, and all the Wrong on the other.

But if that were so, the fact would have appeared in the actual war-aims of these fighters for Right. Self-aggrandisement, territory, markets, nothing of that kind would have been sought by them; for those were the objects of the wicked enemy. For them, Right, Peace, Civilisation, would have been the only motives. They would have had one object, and one only – to disarm, after ending once for all by their victory the reign upon the earth of cupidity and force. Many young men, I think, died in that hope, and in that hope many mothers and wives endured their deaths. Let me cite, once more, an author who was also a combatant:

" 'The freedom of Europe,' 'The war to end war,' 'The overthrow of militarism,' 'The cause of civilisation' – most people believe so little now in anything or anyone that they would find it hard to understand the simplicity and intensity of faith with which these phrases were once taken among our troops, or the certitude felt by hundreds of thousands of men who are now dead that if they were killed their monument would be a new Europe not soured or soiled with the hates and greeds of the old. That the old spirit of Prussia might not infest our world any more; that they, or, if not they, their sons, might breathe a new, cleaner air, they had willingly hung themselves up to rot on the uncut wire at Loos, or wriggled to death, slow hour by hour, in the cold filth at Broodseinde."

So writes Mr. Montague. But how does he continue?

"Now all was done that man could do, and all was done in vain. The old spirit of Prussia was blowing anew; from strange mouths, from several species of men who passed for English – as mongrels, curs, shoughs, water-rugs and demi-wolves are all clept by the name of dogs – there was rising a chorus of shrill yelps for the outdoing of all the base folly committed by Prussia when drunk with her old conquest of France. Prussia, beaten out of the field, had won in the souls of her conquerors' rulers; they had become her pupils; they took her word for it that she, and not the other England, knew how to use victory." [33]

The disillusionment began long before the end of the war, though it was not till the peace treaties that it became confirmed and universal. Meantime, for that disillusionment, a; definite basis was given, to those who were in a position to follow the facts, in the secret treaties, between the Powers of the Entente, published in 1917 by the revolutionary Government of Russia. These treaties had been entered into behind the backs of the combatants. They were "secret," and with reason. For if they had been public they might have chilled to the bone that generous ardour which the conspiring Governments required in their soldiers, that they might achieve purposes the opposite of those which soldiers supposed themselves to be fighting to attain. Let us examine briefly the contents of these treaties, for, though known, they are still too little attended to, and their significance is not properly appreciated. What, as interpreted by these authentic documents, did the Fight for Right really turn out to mean? Did it mean, for example, disarmament, and a world henceforth at peace? Not at all! Of that, not a word in the treaties.

No League of Nations. Nothing whatever hinting even remotely at any change in those motives and policies of statesmen out of which the Great War, like all other wars, had come. Every clause of every treaty dealt simply with the transference of territory from the enemy states to the Allies, that the former might become weaker, and the latter stronger.

Thus, first, Alsace-Lorraine was to be restored to France, without consultation of the inhabitants, without any procedure which could make this transference back to France of a German-born and German-speaking population appear more final or more rightful than its transference from France to Germany in 1870. For (as the Fighters for Right could themselves affirm, when enemy territory was in question) the only test of the rightfulness of a Government is the will of the people to submit to it. I do not say the provinces ought not to have gone back to France, because I daresay (though I do not know) that they would have voted to do so, if they had been consulted. But the taking of the vote would have put upon the fact the seal of a new principle, and that seal the French, from the beginning, refused to give.

This may seem a small point, but it is significant. Let us proceed. By a treaty so secret that it was not communicated even to the English, the French agreed with the Russian Tsardom (that singular champion of Right) to separate from Germany and put under French hegemony all the German provinces on the left bank of the Rhine. Thus the war to avenge the wrong done by Germany to France in 1871 was to issue in a similar wrong, done on a much larger scale, by France to Germany.

British statesmen, their own interest not being concerned, did not approve this arrangement. And it was British as well as American opposition that prevented the French from actually carrying out their policy in the Treaty of Versailles and formally separating the Germans west of the Rhine from Germany. But clearly the French have never abandoned that aim. They have been pursuing it, and are still pursuing it, by other means. Their attitude is perfectly intelligible. It is in harmony with the principles which for centuries have inspired the policy of all states, as they inspired that of Germany in 1870. What it is not in harmony with is the professions of the Allied Powers, who marked themselves off from their enemies as the champions of Right against Wrong. But those professions were intended for a different purpose: they were intended to get the young men to fight. And when their purpose was fulfilled, they could be discarded.

In addition to these spoils on the left bank of the Rhine, France was confirmed by the treaties in her possession of Morocco (an appropriate end to that long story of filibustering to which we have already referred), and was given her share of German colonial territory in Africa, and a part of the Turkish Empire, now at last, after so many years of covetous eyeing by the great Powers, to be partitioned among the representatives of Right.

Not less fortunate was Italy. We have seen how, in the contest for her favour, the Germans and Austrians had been outbribed by the Entente and how she decided that it would pay her better to fight against her allies than to fight on their side. The consideration she was to receive was naturally expressed in terms of territory. She was to have the Trentino (including the purely and patriotically German territory in the South Tyrol), Trieste, and the Adriatic coast and islands; and also her share of the Turkish spoils.

Russia (for the revolution had not yet occurred and

she was still – being under the Tsar – regarded as a friend and an ally in the cause of freedom) was, first, to do what she liked with Poland; and what that would be was pretty well indicated by past history. Poland would be promised autonomy while the war was being fought, and crushed at leisure when it was over. Further, Russia was to receive, at last, Constantinople and the Straits, as well as her share of Turkey. "According to this agreement," writes, in 1922, a Russian historian,[34] "the Ottoman and Austrian Empires were to be divided as spoils of war, Russia receiving Constantinople and the Straits." Exactly. "As spoils of war." The Entente, like the Triple Alliance, had no other purpose or idea.

And England? Oh, England was to have the bulk of the German colonies, and Mesopotamia. Little pickings, hardly worth noticing, when one was fighting for Right!

These treaties, signed between 1915 and 1917, are a sufficient, final, and irrefutable proof of the real objects of the Powers of the Entente. How do they differ from the objects of the Germans and their allies? There is no difference at all. Precisely the thing for which the Germans were held up to the reprobation of the world – their desire to take other people's territory – was the thing, and the only thing, pursued by Germany's enemies. Do you reply that the Turkish Empire deserved and required partition? Perhaps it did. But suppose it had been Germany and Austria that had partitioned it? Those states, if they had won, would certainly have controlled it. Would you have been pleased? And if not, why not? Because they would have mismanaged it? And are you satisfied, then, with the management of Greece, of France, of England, since 1918? No! Your objections to German conquests would have been, simply, that they were conquests by your enemies; as your satisfaction with the conquests of the other Powers is, that they are conquests by yourselves or your Allies. Nothing else ever entered the minds of the Governments fighting the war. All the rest was cant to keep the stream of young men flowing to mutilation and death. And please observe, that in these treaties, there is not even the pretence of the "mandatory" principle to justify the annexations. That was introduced later, under another influence, as was everything else in the final treaties that has any show of a new principle. And that influence came from across the Atlantic. It was the influence of President Wilson and of the United States.

These treaties, then, of the earlier years of the war, are the authentic proofs of the real objects of the Powers of the Entente. And they formed in the end the main part of the final treaties. But there were two important events that caused certain modifications. The first was the Russian Revolution. Of that tremendous event we have not yet seen the end. The first revolution, apparently, was favoured by Great Britain and France. It was hoped it would lead to a more energetic pursuit of the war by Russia. But it was succeeded, in the autumn of 1917, by the second or Bolshevist Revolution. And that was a very different affair. It was a revolution, first against the property system of Europe, secondly against the war and all its works. The Allies of Tsarist Russia were doubly outraged. For first, and chiefly, their property in Russia, including their enormous loans, was confiscated; and secondly, their victory, with all that was to follow it in the way of loot, was endangered. From that time on they were occupied in fomenting civil war in Russia in order to restore their friends, the well-to-do class, to power.

The first effect, then, of the Bolshevist Revolution, was shattering. There was indeed (so it would seem) a moment when the British Prime Minister was contemplating a general peace, which would hand over Russia to the tender mercies of Germany, while securing to France and England what they wanted in the West. But other counsels were adopted, under the influence of the second great fact which had changed the situation. The United States had come into the war, and an attitude different from that of any of the European Governments began now to influence words, if not deeds. For America, and America alone, was disinterested. She was not proposing to get anything out of the war. To her it really was a war for Right. And that view was represented with a simple directness by her President. With his help the war was won, completely and absolutely. The enemy lay prostrate as a great Power had seldom before been prostrate in history. The stage, it seemed, was clear for the bringing into effect of those great principles for which, professedly, the war had been fought. President Wilson came to Europe to secure by his own prestige the results for which, alone, he and his country had fought. And never before has the path of a statesman been followed with such hopes and prayers of all good men, such fears and intrigues of all bad ones. The bad men won the day, for, as is usual, they were cleverer than the good; and America retired, defeated by Europe, to her prewar isolation.

The peace, then, that was finally made was the peace of the secret treaties, modified by the defection of Russia, and camouflaged by that constitution of the League of Nations which, it is pretty safe to say, would never have seen the light of day had it not been given a prominent place, from the beginning, in the programme of President Wilson. Its form, indeed, was rather British than American, for the President's insistence had given power to those elements in England which really did want a better world. But had not the President been there, with his achievement, his honesty, and his determination, Lord Robert Cecil and his friends, I think, would never have had their chance.

But the League of Nations was to be the smallest part of the peace; a mere appendage, leaving untouched all the predatory schemes of the victorious states. The peace was made on the lines of the secret treaties, except so far as Russia, now a pariah, was concerned. Her share of the spoils she had voluntarily renounced; and she had made a separate peace with her enemies. Neither from her own point of view, nor from that of her late Allies, had she any further claim. The division of territory, therefore, could be made without considering her. And the Turkish Empire was distributed between the other Allies – that is, between France, England, Greece and Italy.

There were two other more or less important modifications of the secret treaties. The French claim not only to annex Alsace-Lorraine, but to separate from Germany and put under French domination the whole left bank of the Rhine, met, as we have seen, with strong opposition on the part both of the English and of the Americans. There was a long battle over this point, in which, on the French side, the principal champion was General Foch. Finally a compromise was reached, whereby the occupation of the left bank was to be for fifteen years only, by which time, according to the assumptions of the treaty, Germany would have paid her reparations and would recover her sovereignty. It is clear, however, that from the beginning, the French statesmen were determined that that situation should not arise, and that, in fact, Germany should default, so that their occupation might continue. The following scene is interesting in this connexion. General Foch, supported by M. Jules Cambon and M. Tardieu, had been pressing on the French cabinet his plan for a permanent occupation by the French of the left bank of the Rhine, with power to conscript the German population to fight against their German compatriots. M. Clemenceau was defending, against him, the treaty, as it finally passed, whereby the French have the right of occupation of the left bank for fifteen years only. After explaining how he had been compelled, by pressure from President Wilson and Mr. Lloyd George, to adopt that position, he turned to M. Poincaré, the President, and said: "Mr. President, you are much younger than I. In fifteen years the Germans will not have executed all the clauses of the treaty, and in fifteen years, if you do me the honour to come to my tomb, you will be able to say to me, I am convinced of it, 'We are on the Rhine and we shall stay there.'"

The history of the last few years is one long and terrible comment on these words. You may understand the French attitude – it is only too intelligible – and, understanding, you may approve. But no understanding and no approval can alter facts and consequences. The policy thus adopted means the perpetuation in Europe of fear, hatred and rage; means the new war, when the new conditions arise to make it possible; and means the destruction of civilisation and of mankind. That these men do not see it, will not see it, cannot see it, makes no difference to the fact. M. Clemenceau, as he said, will no doubt be dead before the fruit of his policy matures. M. Cambon and General Foch will perhaps be dead. Those who pay for their error, or their crime, will be a new generation. In ways not fully imaginable by us, and yet imaginable enough, they will fall in holocausts as a sacrifice to the false ideas of these old men, and with themselves they will drag into the abyss all the hopes, all the achievements, and all the promise of mankind. Verily the world pays high for the rule of the old, of the rich, and of the men of fixed ideas!

So much then for France in Europe. Outside, she

took Morocco, as already arranged by the treaties, her share of the German colonies in Africa, and her share of the Turkish spoils.

Turning now to Italy, she was assigned, as by treaty, Trieste, the Trentino, and the South Tyrol. On the Adriatic she was less fortunate. For some reason President Wilson was stiffer here than in other matters; and also the new Yugo-Slav state had to be considered. After long debates and long hovering on the verge of war, a compromise was reached which may or may not be permanent. But if – as Governments and their policies presuppose – the old anarchy is to continue, then there is every chance of war between Italy and the new, ambitious, and inexperienced state that confronts her on the Adriatic.

In the East, Tsarist Russia having disappeared, the Allies felt no further hesitation in "liberating" Poland; not so much from any love of the Poles, as because the French saw in the new state a means of holding both Germany and Russia in check. The new Poland cuts off East Prussia from the rest of the Prussian state, and thus creates a new feud which, when Germany recovers, will hardly be settled without war. Germany has also been deprived of the principal part of the coal supplies of Silesia, whereby the impossibility of her payment of reparations has been increased, and a new source of future wars created.

Austria-Hungary has been disrupted, and the new states carved out of her Empire, while they are dominated by Slavs and Czechs, contain large minorities of Germans and Magyars, who are now the oppressed instead of the oppressors. Meantime, the old Austria is cut off both from the sea and from the neighbouring countries once included in her Empire, and the two million inhabitants of Vienna seem to have little prospect except that of gradual decay by emigration, famine and disease.

But it is on Bolshevist Russia, even more than on Germany, that the full rage of the victorious Powers has been vented. Along her Eastern borders has been created a row of small and (for the moment) independent states. Poland claims another great slice of her territory, inhabited mainly by Jews and Russians. In the East, Japanese troops occupy the Siberian coast.[35] The immense territory of Russia is now almost completely land-locked. And if ever the old governing class regains power, it is as certain as anything can be in history that they will devote themselves to undoing by a new war for empire the results of the "war for liberty."

But strangest of all the fruits of the war is the treatment of the Turkish Empire. To begin with it was partitioned (as by the secret treaties) between England, France and Italy, with a bit added for Greece. For Greece had been secured, it was thought, after long flirting with Germany, for the cause of Right. Meantime, and until further determination, Constantinople and the Straits were to be held jointly by England, France and Italy. From that time on there began a subterranean duel between France and England, which came to a climax in a secret treaty made by the former with Kemal Pasha, who was in rebellion against the Government which both states were nominally supporting at Constantinople. This treaty handed over the Armenians to the Turks, who, during the war, had murdered a million of them in cold blood. It also handed back to Turkey territory which had been entrusted to France under mandate, and was therefore under the control of the League of Nations. The British were taken aback; strong protests were made; and a new treaty agreed to, whereby the Turks were put back into possession of Constantinople and the Bosphorus. Europe, it would almost seem, was unwilling to lose grip of such an ancient and trusty cause of war. There followed the final defeat of the Greeks, morally backed by the British, by the Turks, morally and materially backed by the French. The Turks are now to get Eastern Thrace as well as Constantinople. And the fighters for Right once more endorse the principle that he who takes shall have. In return, the Turks are promising what is called the "freedom of the straits." And it is characteristic of the ways of Governments that this ambiguous phrase is not being defined, at any rate to the peoples concerned. It may mean, as it appears to mean to Mr. Lloyd George, that the straits are to be free to all navies. In that case, it is a war measure, not a peace measure, and one that gives an obvious naval advantage to the British. Or it may mean that in time of peace merchant ships are to be free of the straits. But that they have been for years past. Or it may mean that they shall be so free in war as well as in peace; which is desirable, but probably very difficult to secure, when Turkey is at war. Or it may mean what the Russians are said to be suggesting, that the straits be free to merchant ships but never to warships. And that appears to be the only desirable interpretation and the only one consistent with a genuine intention to end war. By the time this book appears the question will be settled one way or the other.[36] But how characteristic that, at the very moment of its being settled, the peoples of all countries are left so completely in the dark as to what is intended.

So much for the territorial arrangements achieved, after complete victory, in a war for the rights of small nations. All these results, it should be added, are provisional, so that no one can say how much of the structure thus elaborately erected will be left standing ten years hence. Meantime, on another great question – more important in the eyes of the victors than all this rearrangement of Europe – their record was equally remarkable. This question was what is called "reparations." What the origin of the war really was, and what kind of responsibility the Germans had for it, we have already seen. But the official theory of the victors was, of course, and is, that the whole blame rested exclusively on the vanquished. They even compelled them to sign a statement to that effect, as though such signature, extorted by force, could make any difference to the facts. In any case, it could make none to the victors' right to reparation, which was governed by their acceptance, as the general basis of the peace, of

President Wilson's manifesto of January 8, 1918 (the fourteen points), and his later utterances. Only two reserves were made. First, in respect of the "freedom of the sea," on which the Powers reserved their liberty of action; next, with respect to reparations, in the statement that Germany should repay all the damage done to the *civil* population of the allied nations and to their properties by the aggression of Germany by sea, land or the air. There was thus no possibility for the victorious Powers, without breaking their pledged word, to claim the whole cost of the war. Yet this was precisely the first thing done by the British delegates at Versailles; and they yielded only to a telegram of President Wilson, during his temporary absence, vetoing that policy as inconsistent with the terms of the German surrender.[37] Worsted in this first bout, the British and the French did not resign their object. Wild promises had been made at the elections, promises incompatible with the pledged word of the Allied Governments, and these promises must somehow be redeemed. After a long and sordid wrangle, it was decided to include the cost of pensions in the damages to be demanded of Germany. That this was incompatible with the plain sense of the declaration on which the Germans surrendered, I do not think any honest and well-informed man can dispute. In any case, the result was disastrous. For it enabled the victorious Governments to make those impossible claims which have prevented the restoration of Europe for the last four years, and are driving us month by month into social disintegration and ruin.

Do I exaggerate? Let the reader then listen to the judgment not of a mere writer but of a public man of the inner counsels, who has therefore both the opportunity to know and the rare courage to say. It is thus that Signor Nitti, the Italian statesman, writes of the state of Europe in June, 1922.

"In an orgy of violence Europe has been tied to a series of errors which in future years will seem to be the exaggerations of historians. While continental Europe suffers impoverishment and Balkanisation, the victorious states, after disarming the vanquished, are maintaining armies, which, in number and efficiency, exceed those of the peoples which were regarded as the provokers of the war and the artificers of militarism. The attempt to execute treaties impossible of execution necessitates armies of occupation which are not only a moral absurdity but have cost Germany over sixteen hundred millions of gold marks, or considerably more than her pre-war army and navy. France and Italy are not paying their debts to the United States; they are not in a position to pay either capital or interest. On the other hand, the Entente is not only claiming that Germany shall pay for the army of occupation and for the whole of the expenditure arising out of control – a sum which is amounting to an enormous figure – but is demanding as reparations huge indemnities and enormous payments in kind!"

There is the judgment of a realistic statesman on the results of four years of the war for Right and four years of the peace which it secured. But perhaps you are not interested in the views of statesmen and economists. Very well; listen then to an American man of business, certainly not a pro-German.

"One does not need to be pro-anything to see that these treaties were conceived in hatred and malice. In the minds of their makers they had a background of an awful irreparable injury they had suffered. The enemy, terribly powerful in his late strength, barbarous in some of his methods of warfare, potentially capable of future reprisals, was for the time being under the heel of the conquerors. It is perhaps not surprising that hatred, retaliation, burning resentment and unfairness were written into them. When treaties are so made, however, they are not a healing document. Outside of the provision for the League of Nations, there is nothing in the various treaties of Paris that is healing. It is very difficult to see, however, how a continent afflicted with them can recover, until they are rewritten; for that they will be rewritten is inevitable. They have set up political situations as unstable as quicksilver. They have drawn national boundary lines that may be erased like pencil marks. They have created economic situations which must be altered, or whole peoples must economically perish." [38]

This is an American, a banker. You don't trust him? Very well. Take, then, an Englishman; take a General; take a man innocent of business, of economics, of everything except chivalry and romance; take one of the men who helped you to win the war. What does Sir Ian Hamilton say of the treaty?

"Fatal Versailles! Not a line – not one line – in your treaty to show that those boys (our friends who are dead) had been any better than the Emperor's; not a line to stand for the kindliness of England; not one word to bring back some memory of the generosity of her sons."

No! Not a line – not one line – in the treaty, nor in any treaty of peace ever framed. For the General, even now, has not fathomed the full tragedy of war. No war ever fought has ever been ended by anything but a base peace. For war is about base things. It matters little what feelings may have possessed the fighting men. It is not those feelings that determine either the cause or the issue of war. War is about territory, power, and trade, and about nothing else. And the peace of Versailles is but one more proof of that fact. Sir Ian Hamilton is not likely ever to learn this truth. He has devoted to war all his chivalry, all his enthusiasm, all his life. But no devotion of the worshipper alters the character of the god. And war remains, what it has always been, murder for the sake of loot; only now, murder on a scale and with a precision that threatens the very existence of the murderers.

14

That the peace, then, should have been what the peace is, follows from the nature of war, for which, while it continues to be a possibility, peace can be nothing but a preparation. It is interesting to find that, in this matter, as in so many others, our own Prime Minister saw clearly what the facts were. He knew what the peace ought not to be, but he was powerless to make it what it ought to be. For he could not destroy, in a few weeks, the passions which he himself, as a War Minister, had been inflaming for five years. The memorandum he presented to his colleagues at Versailles in the spring of 1919 is worth attending to, for it contains some of the truths this book is endeavouring to enforce, stated by the best of authorities – by the man who has been, in his own person, an instrument of the Evils which followed from neglecting them.

The memorandum begins with a sentence of mere rhetoric, worth citing, however, as a curiosity: "To achieve redress our terms may be severe, they may be stern and ruthless, but at the same time they can be so just that the country on which they are imposed will feel in its heart that it has no right to complain." This is mere nonsense. No country would ever believe that a victorious foe thinks about justice, nor, in fact, does such a foe ever so think; for justice would always penalise the victor as much as his enemy. But a victorious foe might conceivably think about security and peace; and this Mr. Lloyd George, having got rid of the cant which he may have thought necessary, does more or less propose. He objects, for instance, to putting under the dominion of Poles and Czechs and Yugo-Slavs "large masses of Germans clamouring for reunion with their native land." He objects to a similar treatment of Magyars. He sees clearly that that procedure will lead to new wars in East Europe.

Further, he sees the spirit of revolution abroad in every country. "The whole existing order in its political, social and economic aspects is questioned by the masses of the population from one end of Europe to the other." He sees the possibility of an invasion of Europe by the Russian Red Army – "the only army eager to fight because it is the only army that believes that it has any cause to fight for." What a piece of candour is that! And how any "pacifist" or "Bolshevist" would be belaboured if he had ventured to say the same thing! This possibility of an invasion by the Red Army is not made less possible by the fact that the only alternative may be death by starvation – a starvation which the Western Governments, in their desire to destroy Bolshevism, have deliberately and in cold blood refused to alleviate. History, in spite of all its irrationality, has its Nemesis, and we may witness it here.

Mr. Lloyd George proceeds: "The greatest danger that I see in the present situation is that Germany may throw in her lot with Bolshevism, and place her resources, her brains, her vast organising power, at the disposal of the revolutionary fanatics whose dream it is to conquer the world for Bolshevism by force of arms." Three years have passed since those words were written. The Allied Governments have been doing all they could, ever since, to destroy the whole fabric of civilisation and order in Germany. They have not quite succeeded yet. But every day brings the consummation nearer. Already, at Genoa, Germany and Russia have signed an economic treaty. Press them a little harder and they may sign a military one. But if they do, not they, but the policy of the victorious Powers, will be to blame.

Finally, Mr. Lloyd George suggests that it will not be convenient to impose a peace which no responsible German Government would carry out. For what could we do in such a case? We might blockade Germany. But Mr. George professed doubt whether public opinion "would allow us deliberately to starve Germany." Here he was perhaps unduly pessimistic. Public opinion in England, that is, the public opinion that counts – *The Times* and the Georgian Press, rich men and women, and members of Parliament – is quite ready to starve anybody to death, as their attitude towards Russia at this moment shows. It is only the poor and the unemployed, only the negligible nine-tenths of the nation, that object and they can be ignored. But then, the memorandum goes on, even if we did so, the result would only be "Spartacism from the Urals to the Rhine." Yes. And that is what we are waiting for. It stands now at the door.

Seeing then, with a clairvoyance unusual in a statesman, what the results must be of imposing a peace of vengeance, Mr. George counsels a moderate indemnity;[39] the smallest possible transfer of Germans to foreign rule; and, above all, a genuine League of Nations preceded by a large measure of disarmament. "The first condition of success for the League of Nations is a firm understanding between the British Empire and the United States of America and France and Italy that there will be no competitive building of fleets or armies between them. Unless this is arrived at before the covenant is signed, the League of Nations will be a sham and a mockery." Those words are so true that they might have been spoken by a pacifist. They were too true for Mr. George's followers, for the men, that is, who had been elected, on his invitation, to impose a peace of hatred and revenge. The memorandum became known through a newspaper, and instantly the Prime Minister was bombarded by the famous telegram from four hundred of the wolves the election had put into Parliament. There must be no relenting, no weakness, no tenderness to the vanquished foe. Germany must be squeezed (in the famous phrase for which, perhaps, Sir Eric Geddes may go down to immortality) "till the pips squeak." This, probably, would have been enough to recall Mr. George to the paths of insanity, even if there had been nothing else. But there was something else. There was M. Clemenceau. It is characteristic of a war that its popular hero should bear the nickname of the "Tiger." But perhaps the word does not do full justice to M. Clemenceau's qualities. He has indeed the cruelty of the beast of prey. But he supplements it with a cold-blooded rationality such as only human beings can achieve. The instincts of the wild beast, governed by the brain of an able man, make up a very formidable combination. M. Clemenceau coldly pointed out, in response to Mr. Lloyd George, that Germany, having lost Alsace-Lorraine and other provinces, and being burdened with a huge indemnity, would, in any case, be thinking of nothing but revenge; that therefore the only thing to do was to make her revenge powerless; and that therefore Mr. George's plea for a reasonable peace must lapse. Mr. George succumbed. Mr. Wilson (in Mr. Keynes' phrase), was "bamboozled," and once bamboozled could not be "debamboozled," even when Mr. Lloyd George wanted to do it. And we got the "peace" we have got – the subterranean fire smouldering till it is ready to break out into the final conflagration.

15

If you have followed me so far, you will, I think, be prepared to agree with the following statements:

1. The Great War, like all international wars, had for its objects, on both sides, increase of power and seizure of territory.

2. These objects became clear at the Peace Treaty. And they were not in the least affected by what soldiers or civilians may have thought they were fighting for. For what states aim at is to be discovered not by what individuals say or think, but by what Governments do.

3. These objects could not have been pursued by war, unless the states had been armed. But the fact that they were armed became itself an independent cause of war, owing to the mutual fear and suspicion thus engendered.

4. If states continue to pursue the same objects by the same means, it is possible that the human race may cease to exist, and pretty certain that civilisation will be destroyed.

Now, if we were dealing with the affairs of any private person, and if it could be shown to him that a certain course of action must lead inevitably to material ruin and physical destruction, probably he would be induced to alter his course. But there is not so much reason to suppose that, after such a demonstration, nations will alter theirs. For no single person feels responsible for the fate of states, and no one cares about it in the way that everyone cares about his own. The intelligent and the unintelligent alike, the men of good will or of bad will, are equally concerned with private ends. They cast, at most, an occasional glance at public affairs, make their gesture of indifference, approval, or disgust, and hopefully, or hopelessly, leave events to take their course. One man is doing business, another manual labour, another philosophy, another art, and all alike go sweeping on, in a kind of blind fatalism, down the stream that is hurrying them to destruction.

Meantime, rulers blunder along, largely in the dark, following traditional purposes to the accustomed goal and excusing themselves, when catastrophes occur, with the reflection that they could not have acted otherwise, because "public opinion" expected of them the line of action which in fact they have adopted. Governments do not lead and nations do not follow. There is a general slithering into the pit, into which, nevertheless, everybody would say they do not wish to fall.

I do not know, I confess, whether, or how, these conditions can be altered. I am not too hopeful of the kind of demonstration given in this book, because I know how people will listen to an argument, admit it, shrug their shoulders, and resume their avocations as before. I am not too hopeful. But since I have chosen to be an observer and a student, I feel some obligation to point out what might be done to avert destruction by nations that should be intelligent and responsible. In this matter I have indeed nothing new to say, for much more has been thought out than people are prepared to do. The achievement would be, if it were possible, to put behind obvious policies some real conviction and driving power.

The machinery required to save mankind is that of a League of Nations, including all states, and having real power to determine all issues between its members. But what is not commonly understood, even among supporters of such a League, is that the League cannot function unless the states alter their policy. I should be much surprised if there are not many who think, as I have heard a distinguished politician say, that for the British a principal object of the League is to facilitate the maintenance, and even the extension, of the British Empire. That, of course, is absurd. A league of nations means nothing of the kind. A league of nations means the substitution of settlement by agreement for settlement by force, and this can only happen if states consciously and deliberately abandon what hitherto has been the sole motive of their policy, the extension or the maintenance of their territory and their power.

Now, as we have seen in our brief survey of the treaties that ended the war, and as becomes every day more and more evident, states in fact have not abandoned the old view and adopted the new one. They are struggling, all of them, still in the old Nessus shirt of aggrandisement.

Starting, as they did, with the main idea of bleeding white the defeated countries, they have not even been able to agree upon that. The British, with the comparative sanity that comes from an intelligent pursuit of self-interest, desire to fix reparations at a reasonable figure and to set Germany on her feet again as an economic factor. The French desire to keep her feeble economically as well as politically. The French, again, desire to reconstitute Turkey – the murderer of a million Armenians – into a state under her own control, in order that she may exploit the Near East at her leisure. And in this they have succeeded. The British desire at once to maintain the Turk, in order to propitiate the Mahommedan population of the Empire, to weaken him, in order to propitiate those elements of British opinion which object to the murder of Christians, and to exploit the oil of the Middle East. The Greeks, supported by the British, have been fighting in Turkey to appropriate Turkish territory. And by virtue of this division among the Powers who stood for Right, the Power that, more consistently than all others has stood for Wrong, has gained in prestige and authority, has retained Constantinople, and is likely to complete the massacre of its Christian populations, while the Christian Powers – who a year or two ago had the situation in their own hands – look on and idly protest. In Russia, the Governments of the victorious states stand by with cold hostility while millions of people perish of famine. They will do nothing until the Russian Government recognises debts which everybody knows that in fact they can never pay; while the Powers bent on extorting from them this admission know also, and know that everyone knows, that they cannot and will not pay their own debts. In the Far East, Japan maintains her illegitimate occupation of Russian territory,[40] and fosters, for her own ends, Chinese anarchy. Throughout the length and breadth of the world there is no sign that the crusaders for Right have any intention of adopting for the future any other course of conduct than that which landed them in the Great War.

To see all this, and to state it, is unfortunately easy enough. Nor is it difficult, in general terms, to point to the remedy. But when one asks why the remedy is not adopted, one is met by a harder problem. Is it simply the wickedness or stupidity of Governments? Probably not. Probably Governments are more intelligent and better than Parliaments. For seldom, I suppose, have collections of men so ignorant, short-sighted, hard-hearted and bad-willed been got together as those composing the present[41] Parliaments of England and France. They are the ripe fruit of five years of war and war propaganda, and there they sit, unrepentant, perpetuating all the follies and all the crimes of that carnival of Evil. But then, granting that Governments are tied by their Parliaments, what ties these? Or, if you like, what gives them their evil freedom? The constituencies? We shall know that better after an election. The constituencies may have changed their minds since the time when they filled with these men the assemblies that rule their country, and thereby let loose upon the world the evils from which it is perishing. Anyhow, it is the constituencies that do, by omission or commission, determine policy, and thereby the fate of that civilisation which they are rather letting run down than actively pushing into the pit.

It is to the electors, therefore, that is to ordinary men and women, that I have addressed these pages; and to those of them who may read me I wish to point out that, although foreign affairs are only part of the problem we have to meet, they are, for the time being, the principal part. For the evils from which we are suffering are the result of our war policy and our peace policy. It will be a long time before any real reforms at home can be undertaken, though no doubt revolution may be precipitated. Some would wish to do this; and I do not propose now to argue that point. For most people it will be enough to look at Russia. For the evil that has fallen upon her would be as nothing to that which must overwhelm an industrial state like England, dependent for its bare existence on foreign trade. Revolution is possible, and may be brought upon us by the kind of policies Governments are pursuing; but it could only be a form of suicide.

Any movement, not revolutionary, that proposes to do good, must start with the condition of Europe and of the world. And what it must aim at is clear enough to all thinking men, though not, for that reason, easy to achieve. The German indemnity must be fixed, and fixed at a possible sum; and a moratorium must be granted. The foreign troops, which are eating up the greater part of what Germany has hitherto contributed, must be withdrawn from her territory. Germany must be admitted to the League of Nations. The Russian Government must be recognised, and that country too, if it will, be admitted to the League. The Supreme Council of the Allies must cease to exist and the League become the sole channel for the conduct of international affairs.

16

The brief programme stated in the last section, and advocated, for months and years past, by everyone who can understand and feel and desire rightly, sums up what ought to be done at once, and what must be done, if civilisation is to be saved. Next year, or the year after it may be too late. For we are drawing every month, every week, every day nearer to the edge of the abyss. But if we do succeed in pulling up, and averting immediate ruin, there remains a long and difficult process of conversion before our course can be set permanently in the right way. For we must learn to change altogether our traditional view of our relation to other states and other peoples. Some words I must say on this subject, though I have nothing new to say.

So far as the mass of the people is concerned, those who do the manual and much of the mental work of the world, this conversion would perhaps mainly be a matter of attention. They will have to cease being the prey of patriotic phrases. For that purpose, even a little knowledge would suffice, if it were accompanied by clear perception. What has been said in these few pages would be a sufficient lesson in the real meaning of war to anyone who would let it penetrate his mind. It is this penetration that is the difficulty. In the midst of the fatigue and anxiety of work, the bellowing of the daily press, the claims of the "pictures," of betting and of sport, amid the work and the distraction of life, there is hardly room for a conviction of the most simple and vital truth to penetrate. But once it did penetrate, it would perhaps find the ordinary man ready enough to accept it. For it would be easy to convince him, if he would only look, that, whoever may gain by war and war-preparedness, he is losing all the time. It is he who goes as the common soldier to be slaughtered. It is he who returns, if he does return, to unemployment, semi-starvation and all the evils from which the mass of people have been suffering since the war ended. There is no single good of the common man which is served by war. There is no evil which is not brought upon him by it. And this I think many of them already see, and all might be made to see if they could be induced to attend. But if they were really converted, then wars would cease to occur; for those who make them would have lost the material upon which they work.

There remain, however, and there are likely to remain, for a long time, the comparatively influential people who form or control Governments. Some of these are the professional soldiers and sailors who are set apart to prepare the mechanism of war. So far as these men affect policy they are bound to affect it in the direction of war. I do not libel them in saying this. The other day I heard Lord Haldane speak on this topic. He expressed, to begin with, enthusiasm for the character of soldiers as he had met them when he was Secretary for War. But he went on to say that, if you give control of policy to soldiers, and in proportion as you do so, you will have war.

The late war he regarded as produced by the militarism of Germany and Austria. But a similar danger, he said, exists in all countries wherein the military element is allowed to dictate policy. I cite Lord Haldane, because he has been in a position to prove by experience this truth, which is, however, evident without it. For even if we do not attribute to soldiers any love of war, their business is to forestall by force danger from force. Soldiers thus imply armaments and think in terms of armaments. It is they who push on the continual growth of armies and navies, of aeroplanes, of poison gas, of all the mechanism of destruction. And, as we have seen, that very growth becomes itself a principal cause of war. A soldier may be by nature the most admirable of men. I will not dispute it. But his mind suffers almost of necessity, from a fundamental warping, which makes of him an agent of destruction.

The more professional soldiers, the more armaments; and the more armaments the more and the worse war.

This is a simple truth that anyone can grasp, once it has been stated, without elaborate education or knowledge. Look round, for instance, at this moment upon the world. Look no nearer than across St. George's Channel. At the moment of my writing these words, society in Ireland is disintegrating. Life is not safe, property is not safe. And why? Every Irishman carries arms, and therefore a fanatic is able, as he is willing, to murder political opponents, instead of conferring with them. On the other hand, the police force, the usual guarantee of order, does not act in that capacity. The vendetta is either fostered or endured by the authorities. Disarm the individual citizens in Ireland, and use your police force properly, and that feature of the situation would disappear. Well, it is just the same among states. For example, ever since the armistice, there has been actual or potential war between Poland and Russia. Why? Because both sides have had armed forces watching one another, or attacking one another. There were causes of dispute, of course, apart from the forces. But if there had been no forces there would have had to be, sooner or later, settlement by consent. For though people will kill one another rather than compromise, they will not indefinitely live in un-exciting discomfort and disorder without even the chance of ending that by murder. The only answer I know of to these considerations, would be: we prefer to live armed, in order that we may kill one another, rather than compromise. And if that is really anyone's view, I have no more to say. I merely invite him to face the real facts.

You may retort, perhaps, "Yes, that would be all very well, if we had only the 'civilised' nations to think of. But there is the great world outside. For example, there are Africans." Yes! And what are we doing to Africans? The French are deliberately conscripting and training them in our methods of warfare in order to bring them to Europe to fight Europeans I If ever primitive peoples get strong enough to be a menace to those we call "civilised" it will be because the civilised have taught them. The injustices and cruelties of white men to black, long continued and still continuing, form one of the most horrible chapters of history. But, at least, compared to whites, the blacks are powerless. It is not from their strength that the problem of war arises. It is only by the deliberate folly and crime of white men that they can ever be a menace to them; only by training them, that is, to take part in our wars.

But China? Ah! What a story is there, not here to be retold! China is the only peaceable nation there has ever been. If she be driven to be a "menace" it will be our doing. For only by us, the strong states, supplying her, for our purposes, with our guns, our generals, and our training, could that menace ever take effect. True, that is just what we are doing, what especially Japan is doing. But let us not put the blame on China. If we chose to disarm, instead of arming China, there could be no trouble in China that could menace the world, even if China wished to make it. And of all nations she is the least likely to wish it. For her people, and perhaps hers alone, are naturally pacific.

Why then, I repeat, can we not disarm? Is it the armament firms? Those gentlemen, no doubt, desire to perpetuate war that they may make profits. Very likely they do all they can to influence opinion, as well as policy, in that direction. Every now and again one comes across instances of their activities, pursued though they be mostly in the dark. And no doubt also the men they employ, by an ironic necessity of their position, would be opposed to the scrapping of their industry. But after all, this objection, though not negligible, could be met easily enough. In Germany the armament firms are devoting themselves now to other forms of production. They would do the same here. And as to the workmen, it would be much cheaper to pension them off, if they were thrown out of work, and to pay them for doing nothing, than to keep them employed on armaments. The raw material, at any rate, would be saved, and if they made nothing useful, they would at least cease from turning out tools of destruction. This question of the armament firms would not be a serious argument against a real determination to disarm, although it might be – and no doubt is – an additional force working along with inertia, stupidity, fear and bad will, to stop disarmament.

"But still," you will insist, "we must not disarm. For disarmament would not give *absolute* security. Some state might always run amuck and make a sudden raid with aeroplanes, or something of the kind." Really, men are very odd creatures! They think, in panic, of all the possible evils of conditions hitherto untried. But they face, with complete indifference, evils far worse which all experience shows to follow from conditions tried. "If we continue to arm, we shall certainly perish." "Well, perhaps!" and a shrug of the shoulders. "Disarm then!" "Ah no – for that would not be *quite* safe!"

Why, I must ask, do you feel safer when frontiers are bristling with forces, all ready at any moment to be let loose, than when (as, for example, along the frontier of Canada and the United States) there are no forces? Why? Are more people likely to be killed in the one case than in the other? Or can it be that, being elderly civilians, you like to think that the young men will be there, in the armed world, all ready to be killed and to save you, whereas in the disarmed world, it might be you, who suffered? I do not wish to be offensive, but really, is that it?

"No," you say indignantly. "The real point is, that in the world supposed to be disarmed, the *others* might cheat." (We, of course, never should.) Very well. Then what do you say to this? Constitute an international air-force and an international fleet, openly and above board, as a police force, to meet any such possible raid from some imagined dishonest state. "No! We wouldn't trust that." Heavens! the things you will trust, and the things you won't. You will "trust" the arrangement that has produced war after war and must destroy civilisation and mankind, and you won't trust any arrangement, however sensible, that might save you. Why? Is it mere stupidity and conservatism?

There is a great deal of that. But we must recognise that that is not all. The truth is, that men are not thinking only of defence when they insist on maintaining armaments. They are thinking also of freedom to do what they like to people weaker than themselves. They are thinking of objects that can only be obtained by force. I have said, what is true, and what all history shows to be true, that no state hitherto has had any policy except that of taking territory and markets from other states. I have shown that this statement, so far from being refuted, has been illustrated, on a huge scale, by the treaties that followed the war for liberty. Well, this policy, now still that of all states, is the real bottom cause why states will not disarm.

17

Let us examine a little the way in which this motive of cupidity works now, in our own time; for at different periods in history it has taken different forms. At the present time it appears as the economic ambition of great financial corporations. It is not, however, very easy to get this issue faced frankly by the ordinary citizen. For it is commonly mixed up with socialist propaganda, and to most men who are not socialists any argument advanced by socialists, however palpably true, is disregarded as a kind of wickedness. Besides, the capitalist groups very likely are not themselves consciously desiring war, nor perhaps even clearly perceiving that their desires will end in war. They are pursuing what presents itself to them as a purely business policy. But they are pursuing it by pressure on Governments, and in the expectation of support from Governments. They ally themselves, in this, with the simpler imperialism of soldiers and adventurers, till finally a situation is produced in which it is possible to appeal to that blind patriotism of the ordinary man which has always been at the service of any Government, in any cause, so long as the cause is properly presented. And so to present it is the business of the press and the politicians.

It will be most useful to take one or two concrete cases of the way in which the economic interest of powerful groups leads states into war. Let us take Mexico. For many years past British and American Combines have been contending to secure control over the oil fields in that territory. They have supported one Government, and opposed another. They have inspired filibustering expeditions by land and sea.

As a well-informed French writer puts it: "The Mexican republic passed its days in peace so long as the dictator Porfirio Diaz reserved all railway and oil concessions for the Harriman and Rockefeller Trusts; but immediately the legal Government displayed its intention of negotiating with European groups as well, civil war broke out. Extemporary generals, lawyers on the make, placed themselves with their bands in the pay of the rivals, and were duly supplied with money and munitions, the one across the land frontier and the others through the gulf ports. Any brigand chief lucky enough to threaten Tampico was sure of getting subsidies and arms from one side or the other. It was the period of *pronunciamentos* in the Spanish style, in which the gold of the British and American Trusts played a barely disguised part. The struggle still goes on; the recent assassination of Carranza was only an incident in it. Rockefeller and Lord Cowdray continue to make war on each other, with the help of Mexican *condottieri*; and impassioned discussions of the different constitutional programmes only hide at bottom the opposing interests of the Standard Oil and the Mexican Eagle." [42]

Hitherto, largely through the peaceful policy of

President Wilson, the oil interests have failed to produce their war. But very possibly it will come soon. When it does, watch it. You will find that some episode will occur which will be represented by the press – prompted by the oil interests – as an insult to the American flag, as an outrage on American citizens, as one of those things that immediately stir the pugnacious instincts of the ordinary man. He will begin to cry for satisfaction – of course through the mouth of the press – and the cry will spread like an infectious disease. Finally, the ultimatum will be presented, the forces raised, the invasion consummated.

Months and perhaps years of hideous guerrilla war will follow, passions getting more and more inflamed the while, atrocities becoming more terrible, and reason, humanity and common sense retiring every day before the flood of hatred. Then, at last, the Americans will be victorious. They will annex Mexico. And the only people who will profit will be the shareholders of the oil-combine – if indeed even they profit. Because, in the course of the war, most likely the oil fields will have been devastated as they were, for instance, in Roumania during the late war.

Thus much the ordinary outsider can learn, or safely infer, about Mexico and the United States. But there is much he cannot learn, because such intrigues are carried on as secretly as possible. It is quite possible that the directors of the Standard Oil Trust, or of Dutch-Shell, might express moral indignation at the notion that they were fostering war; it is even possible that they might feel it. They would perhaps say they were only standing on their "Rights." And, of course, if that happens to involve a war, they cannot help it!

We will take another case more pertinent to the British Empire. In one respect that Empire, in the past, has pursued a comparatively sane policy; after annexing by force a quarter of the globe, it has, on the whole, during the last half century or so, avoided the snare of pursuing a monopoly of trade and raw materials. But of late years ominous signs have been appearing of a different policy. Thus in 1919 there was imposed, on palm kernels from British West Africa, a differential duty on all exports to countries lying outside the Empire, with the view of securing the whole product for England, in order that the oil seeds might be crushed there and there only. "If," said a Minister, "a duty of £2 per ton be found insufficient to divert the trade to this country, the amount should be raised until the duty is adequate to effect its purpose; and this determination should be made clear from the outset." "This duty," says a well-informed writer, "was imposed not in the interests of the colonies but in the supposed interests of a small group of manufacturers within the British Commonwealth." Now observe! The immediate effect was to penalise the native producer. He got less for his produce, because the British manufacturer was given a monopoly of its purchase. It was, perhaps the first open attempt of recent years, though it may not be the last, to exploit the native producer in the interests, or supposed interests, of the British manufacturer. And it is with the greatest satisfaction that those who care for peace will have noted the abolition of the differential duty in 1922. It was, however, then stated, by the Undersecretary for the Colonies, that the object for which it had been originally imposed, the diversion to England of the trade in an "empire product," had been achieved. And if that is so, those who believe in running the Empire as a monopolistic concern are likely to revert to similar policies. It is therefore worth while to point out that such policies are war-policies. For in consequence of them it can be represented, to and by capitalists and Governments, that the political ownership of territory is essential to economic prosperity; that, therefore, the ownership of such territory by another state is an injury to one's own state: that, therefore, one must fight other states in order that one's own state may be, or become, the owner. And that opinion, together with armaments, is a principal cause of modern wars. It is for that reason that Morocco, for example, nearly produced a European war in 1905 and 1911. The French, assisted by their allies, were determined to secure the political control of that country in order to exploit it economically. The Germans not unnaturally objected. Similarly with Persia. The Russians and British divided that country into "spheres of influence" and decided that all public works, such as railways, should be carried out only by the capital and industry of the two interested nations. Once more Germany objected. Was it not natural? In every part of the world, yet unexploited and unowned by the industrial states, one finds, for years past, and progressively in the last ten years, these motives controlling policy. They are primarily the motives of capitalistic groups. But those groups have influence with Governments. And they associate with themselves the more disinterested passions of soldiers and adventurers, to whom it is a kind of axiom, self-evident, that it is somehow good that their country, and not some other, should acquire by force anything that is going in the world.

The motive of profit thus illustrated may be found lurking under many of the wars of recent years. It was a strong element in the Tripoli war, in the war with the Matabele in South Africa, engineered by Cecil Rhodes, in the Russo-Japanese war (where the prize was to be the exploitation of China). It is not indeed the sole cause of war. Into some wars, such as those in the Balkans, it has perhaps hardly entered at all. But it was a considerable part of the causation of the great European war. For, firstly, previous friction in Europe, for example over Morocco, or Persia, was due to it, in whole or in part; and, secondly, the desire of the British to ruin German trade, under the mistaken idea of benefitting their own, though it was not strong enough by itself to engender the war, was one of the contributory rills that fed the great torrent. In the peace treaties this economic notion became very prominent. For those treaties gave the victorious Powers the right, which they have exercised ruthlessly, to expel their German rivals, by force, from their possessions and their businesses over a great part of the world. Yes! the reader may hear, if he listens carefully, behind the patriotic cries of the press, behind the shrieks of wounded and dying men, giving their lives, as they think, for freedom and their country, the cold miscalculations of business men risking the certainty of general loss for small possibilities of individual gain.

18

Very well. But, this being true, what are you going to do about it? Are you going to prefer, at some given moment, your personal profit, with the chance of war looming in the distance, to your personal loss, or the absence of your gain, for the sake of peace? It is really, at bottom, in these kind of terms that the question comes up for many of us. For instance, you were interested, let us say, in the Co-operative Wholesale Society. That society was profiting, let us suppose (I do not know whether it was, but it conceivably might be), by the export duties, which gave the monopoly of crushing palm kernels from West Africa to British firms. We will suppose, for the sake of argument, that in consequence you got some small pecuniary profit. Suppose you did, would you have been willing to vote for abolishing that policy (which makes for war) at the cost of losing that profit? Would you? It is really in that form that ultimate political questions should be put to an elector, if they were put fairly. Or again: you are a share-holder, let us say, in the company which has something like a monopoly of the oil of Mesopotamia.

Are you prepared to abandon this advantage for the sake of peace? It is not, I know, so simple as all that, but at bottom it is something like that. Is your personal advantage of more value to you than the peace of the world? Or we will put it another way. Are you determined to look only to the point of your personal advantage, hoping – perhaps not even dishonestly, perhaps only lazily – that the consequences to the peace of the world may not really result, and pretending that, anyhow, you are not responsible?

I put this matter as one for the individual elector, as a conflict between his interest and his love of peace, or, which is the same thing, between his short-sighted view of his own advantage, and the real advantage, in the long run, of his children, his fellow citizens, and, really, of himself. If political questions could be so put and so judged, we should at least know where we are. But they are never put so simply, they are put in a fog of confusion, misrepresentation and passion. The Imperialist, especially (and he will long be with us) prefers fog, both for himself and for others. For in the fog flourish, like fungi, the strong and irrational emotions on which he lives. All sorts of mean, short-sighted interests of individuals and of groups associate themselves with his propaganda. But at bottom it has a kind of fuliginous disinterestedness. He just wants (and he would think it a kind of blasphemy to question the goodness of his want) to belong to something very big, very strong and able, billing to assert its will by force against all other beings. Such an attitude means war. And such people will never be induced to face the fact of what war is. If ever they think of peace, they imagine it, vaguely, as somehow established by a British

Empire imposing itself on the world. And as that is a very remote ideal, it does not trouble them in their actual pursuit of war. The fact that war, under modern conditions, must mean the end of the British Empire, along with all the rest of what we call civilisation, does not alarm them, for they refuse to look at it. "After me, the deluge. The Empire is my creed."

These are the kind of men we have to deal with. But their only strength is what they derive from their influence with you. It is your hesitation, between this kind of thing and the argument I am advancing, that keeps everything in suspense, and hangs us all over the abyss.

At this moment, for instance, there is proceeding (I do not know whether to success) a campaign for what is called Imperial "preference." What does this really mean? It means that the states of the British Empire, owning a quarter of the globe and an enormous proportion of its raw products (though in that Empire there are only some sixty million white men) desire to make, so far as they can, of that portion of the globe, a closed preserve. But to do that is, quite plainly, to invite a combination of other states against the British Empire, and to prepare another world war. This argument will leave an Imperialist cold. He will, first of all, pooh-pooh it; and then, when it is pressed home, say to himself in his own heart: "Well, why not? That is the price of Empire." Yes, and it is also the end of mankind. You do not like these summary statements?

No. But it is they, and they alone, that bring out the essential facts. And it is the refusal to face these facts that leads us on to catastrophe.

19

The arguments of the preceding sections lead us, quite simply and inevitably, to certain principles of international policy which must be adopted by all states, and especially by the British Empire, if there is ever to be peace in the world. They may be summed up in the following rules to which the members of a true league of nations would have to subscribe:

First, that they will not impose anywhere in their dominions, and least of all in their colonial territories, any duties intended to favour any state, even though it were their own state, against other states.

Secondly, that they will not endeavour to secure for themselves or their friends a monopoly or any special preference in raw materials, such as oil, or iron, or gold, or cotton, or phosphates, or anything else; but, on the contrary, will agree either to sell all such things openly to those, of any nationality, that will pay best for them; or, in the case of necessities, of which the supply is limited, to distribute them, on some equitable principle, among those who have need of them.

Thirdly, that they will not give any special advantage to their own nationals to invest capital, and get contracts, anywhere in their own territories, but will permit a genuine free bidding on the part of all nationalities.

If this policy were adopted, the ownership of territory would become, what it ought to be, a responsibility without advantage; states would cease to compete for it; and the principal cause of wars would be removed.

Now these propositions thus briefly laid down may possibly receive a kind of lazy assent from many readers whose interests are not immediately involved. But many of those who understand their implications, would (if they thought there was any chance of their being adopted) be filled with a genuine rage. For to many Imperialists and to many members of the profit-making classes, it is a matter of course that an Empire exists, if not solely, yet in part, to put money into the pockets of the people at home. I will cite only one sentence, uttered in Parliament, and expressing the real, almost instinctive view of many well-to-do men: "The land belongs to the Empire, does it not? And the people who live on it grow nuts, do they not? If a man or a nation own the land, and has to look after the people who live on it, and protect them from the Germans or other barbarians, it is perfectly right that that man or nation should have the first or a better chance of buying the nuts off that land than anybody else." This discourse of nuts gives the whole argument in a nutshell. Whether the gentleman thus speaking knew that what he was advocating was the perpetuation of war to the destruction of mankind, I do not know. But it is not likely; for such men (who are average and typical men) do not think of the remoter consequences of their principles. But there can be no reasonable doubt that the first stage must lead to the last. Let territory be seized for that purpose, and held in that spirit, and there can never be peace in the world. But, as I have abundantly shown, and as no one really ventures to dispute, the continuance of war means the end of civilisation, if not of mankind.

20

The account I have given in the previous pages of the causes of war between states is, I believe, true and complete. But there is another kind of war – the war called "civil." It has been waging, or is now waging, in many countries since the Great War; in Russia principally; but also in Hungary, in Germany, in Ireland. In Italy, the fighting between *fascisti* and socialists is a mild form of it.[43] It is a fire burning under ground, and sometimes breaking out on the surface, in almost all the states of the world. And, plainly, its causes are different from those of international war. For some reason, not very easy to understand, once one has begun to think about it, civil war is commonly regarded as something much worse than international war. It has, no doubt, all the evils that attach to all war, and those evils, in this case, cannot be thrust out of sight into some other country, where they are not felt by those who maintain the war. That perhaps is why it is thought to be worse than foreign war. But in fact it is, in one important respect, better. It is usually about something that really matters to those who wage it. This fact is clearest in the case of social revolutions, where the object is to better the position of oppressed classes. In our time, the greatest example of that is the Russian revolution. I cannot, in this place, discuss these wars which arise from intolerable misgovernment by privileged minorities. They are altogether different from the international wars with which I am at present concerned, and it is possible that they may fill the near future with events at present undreamed of. For the demoralisation caused by foreign war is the readiest cause of civil war, and of that demoralisation we have our fill. I will therefore only say, in passing, that the experience of the Russian revolution holds out little hope that any result other than final destruction could be attained by similar movements in the western European states. For these, and especially England, are far more dependent on foreign trade than ever Russia was, and far less capable of surviving its collapse. Yet even in Russia millions have perished, and are perishing, of famine.

The civil wars of which I wish to speak are those more intimately connected with my immediate subject. They are those where a people, included by force under a Government to which they object, endeavours to throw off its rule. These wars, if they have been successful, have commonly received the approval of historians, unless the historian belongs to the country against whom the rebellion took place. Thus, for example, the wars of Italy against Austria are usually praised, though not by Austrians. So are the wars of the Poles against Russians, though not by Russians; and so are the Irish "rebellions," though not by Englishmen. For most states disapprove of the oppression of a people by other states, though approving such oppression by themselves. For when they do it themselves they do not admit that it is oppression.

Now what has to be said, first, about these wars, is this. The peoples now striving to free themselves were enslaved originally by international war. They were once free, and then were made by force part of another state. It is thus, for example, that Poland was partitioned, that Korea was seized by Japan, that Ireland or India was taken by England. Such acts of violence, the consequence and the object of international war, seldom result, even after years and centuries, in a real acquiescence on the part of the conquered people. Ireland, Poland, the Slav and Czech peoples of the old Austro-Hungarian Empire, are familiar illustrations of this fact. We begin, now, to see the same thing in India and Egypt, and it will perhaps not be long before the black races of Africa give us another proof. International war, evil in every other respect, produces also the specific evil that it engenders what are called civil wars.

Now the late war, though, as we have seen, it originated in the lust for power on the part of states, in their ambitions and their consequent fears, has, nevertheless, done something towards setting free oppressed peoples. It has reconstituted Poland, and it has detached from the Austro-Hungarian Empire the Slav and Czech and Italian peoples. It has also, no doubt, included, against their will, in the new states, reluctant minorities of the races formerly dominant.

This is especially true of the new Roumania, the new Czech-Slovakia and the new Poland; and it is also true of Italy, which has included in its boundaries the Germans of the Tyrol. Still, when all is said, the states of the new Europe are nearer than those of the old to being what are called "national" states.

Will this be a good thing? No one can yet say. For everything depends on the behaviour of these new states. There are two dangers before them. First, that of aggressive patriotism. It is a commonplace of history that no sooner has a state liberated itself from oppression than it starts out to oppress others. We see this everywhere; in Athens and Sparta, for example, when they had saved themselves from the Persians; in Spain, when it had thrown off the Moors; in France, when it had expelled the English. Even the new Italy has produced its jingos, urging that a successful nationalism must be followed by an aggressive imperialism. And we have yet to see whether America, now, and perhaps for many centuries to come, the strongest state in the world, will be able to resist this temptation.

The first danger, then, to peace, caused by the creation of the new states, is that they may become Imperialist. There is nothing new to be said about this; it will be merely the taking up by the new states of the bad traditions of the old ones. And these new states, being inexperienced, may now be a greater menace than the old.

But there is another danger. These new states, as we have seen, include recalcitrant minorities of different races who object to being held under their rule. This will be a source of new wars, unless the policy of the new states is going to be better than that of the old empires, out of which they have been formed. Besides this, there is the ambition of the old states that have been destroyed to recover their territories. Thus, in Hungary, large numbers of people appear to be possessed by the idea of a war of revenge and recovery.

It is difficult to estimate the force of these motives for war. Everything will depend upon the behaviour of the new states, first to other states, and next to the alien minorities included in their populations. But some observations are worth making. First, experience has shown that it was a mistake (though it may have been one unavoidable) to create new states in absolute sovereignty, instead of making it a condition of their recognition that they, in their turn, should recognise obligations to one another. We come here upon one of the worst prejudices which attach to the theory and the passions of states; the prejudice that it belongs to their nature, and is essential to their self-respect, that they should not be bound, in their conduct to other states, by any rules other than such as they choose to adopt themselves. This theory, supported by these passions, is commonly called "sovereignty." And it is time that it was abandoned. No state ought to be sovereign, for every state ought to be bound by rules, governing its relations to other states, which it cannot alter without their consent. For instance, it should have been (as we have said) a condition of the recognition of the new states formed out of the Austrian Empire that they should trade freely with one another, instead of setting up the wall of tariffs which has done so much, during the last few years, to increase the misery of that part of the world. If the reply be, as very likely it may be, that the states would not have accepted such a condition, that only shows how the idea of sovereignty, and the passions behind it, lies at the root of many of our troubles. The old Austro-Hungarian Empire, with all its grave defects, did at least maintain an economic union throughout a great part of East Europe. Its disruption, in destroying that, has introduced a flood of new evils.

It is then, to begin with, a condition of a better order in the world, that this theory of sovereignty should be modified. The theory, of course, is that of International Law. But it is built upon an emotional fact, and that fact is the pride of nations. They hate to be bound by anything except their own imperfect, aggressive, and usually unjust will. If this attitude is to continue, war will continue. But in fact the attitude is being modified. The League of Nations, for example, though it does not directly contravene national sovereignty, does nevertheless undermine it, and rightly so. Again, what is the position of the self-governing dominions in the British Empire? Are they "sovereign?" I fancy that they would say so. But, if so, sovereignty means something different from what used to be implied by the word. Or again, what about the new Egypt? That state is subject, in foreign policy, to the control of England.

Yet the British Government officially declares it to be "sovereign." Sovereignty is clearly becoming more and more indefinite in its meaning. That that indefiniteness should continue and increase, until the word has lost all meaning, would be the best augury of a world intending to keep the peace.

One of the most important cases in which the sovereignty of states has been encroached upon, in the recent settlement of Europe, is that which concerns the position of minorities of alien races. The new states created by the war have signed an agreement that they will treat such minorities fairly in matters of education, religion and the like; that they will not, in fact, penalise them for being alien. To say this is one thing, to do it another. But that it should have been said is something, perhaps much. Moreover, if the obligation is not complied with, the minorities can appeal to the League of Nations.

Such legal obligations, it is true, are only of value if the states concerned live up to them. But they do, in themselves, set up a pressure in their own favour. We need not be dupes. We have not, merely by words, secured deeds. Yet at least we have written down in black and white that the deeds ought to be. That is something. How much it is, the future will show. And what the future shows will be whether or no one of the causes of war is to persist. For it was the treatment of Croats and Serbs by Hungarians that was part cause of the war of 1914. And the treatment of Germans by

Czecho-Slovaks, or of Magyars by Roumanians, or of Lithuanians by Poles, may be part cause of another and final Armageddon.

On this question, then, of nationality, the truth seems to be as follows:

1. It is desirable that, so far as possible, people belonging to a single nation should be grouped together in a self-governing body.

2. This self-government, however, need not be and should not be absolute. It should be limited by the common needs and obligations of all states, as expressed in the covenant, and the subsequent agreements, of a league of nations. States ought not to be "sovereign" in the old sense of that term. Their absolute freedom should be progressively limited by the needs of the world.

3. Where (as, of necessity, in many parts of Europe must be the case) people of one race are included in a state controlled by another, these minorities should be given guarantees against oppression, and those guarantees should be put under the guardianship of the League of Nations. Actually, in the case of the new states, this has been done.

21

At this point, since I am speaking to Englishmen, it may be worth while to say a few words about what is called the British Empire. The name is only partially appropriate. For the greater part of the area of the Empire is occupied by white men, connected only by the loosest political tie with Great Britain. So far, the "Empire" is a union of free communities, and might more properly be termed, as it sometimes is, the British Commonwealth. On the other hand, the greater part of the population is included in what really is an Empire, for it is governed not by itself, but by British administrators.

Now there are certain policies that might be adopted by this huge agglomeration that would be definitely war-policies. One of these is what is called imperial preference. I have already spoken of this, and shown how the attempt to make of an area of one quarter of the globe, spread dispersedly over its surface, a closed preserve for British citizens, must make the Empire a target for the hostility of all other states. And it is noticeable that an argument sometimes used in favour of that policy is precisely that it would make the Empire stronger in war. Here, as always, the anticipation of war prompts policies that cause war. The notion that we have a "right" to adopt Imperial preference proceeds from that theory and passion of sovereignty which I have already discussed. We have the right only by a bad and dangerous tradition. Such Rights are Wrongs from the point of view of civilisation and mankind. And only a recognition of that fact can save us from destruction.

I turn next more particularly to the Empire proper, as distinguished from the Union of Dominions peopled by white men. The Empire, in this restricted but accurate sense, comprises some four hundred million people, black or brown or yellow, who are governed, more or less autocratically, by England. This is apt to be, I will not say forgotten, but ignored, when we boast of our free Empire. But it is a fact, and one of the most difficult facts with which we have to deal.

On this subject I have, here and now, only one thing to say. The justification of our position as rulers would be that we should put first the interests of the native peoples, and second our own; and that as, or if, from our education and our rule, they begin to claim the right of self-government, we should gladly and freely concede it. For since Empire, properly understood, would be a burden and not a profit, we might be glad enough to lay it down when the people we had ruled were ready to take it up. If all the European states accepted, in practice, that principle, which they are apt to profess to accept in theory, it is clear that they would never make wars among themselves to take territory in Africa or Asia. That they do make such wars shows that they expect to profit by what they take. The record of no state in this matter is very clean. It shows that all of them have taken the territories of primitive men mainly for the sake of the profit they expected to make, either in Imperial defence, or in trade and finance, or both. Why else did the French take Morocco? Why else the British Egypt? Why else the partitioning of the German colonies in Africa among the victors? For the pretence that their only object was to deliver the natives from German oppression is the kind of hypocrisy one wonders that statesmen think it worth while to maintain, seeing that nobody believes them, any more than they believe themselves.

On this tremendous and tragic theme of cruelty and crime, we cannot here digress. But this is to be said. So long as the ownership of African and Asiatic territory is regarded as a pecuniary or military advantage to the owning state, so long will competition for those territories be a cause of war. The system of "mandates" was intended to put an end to that. It might succeed, if it were taken seriously and honestly. There, too, as yet, the balance hangs trembling. If the mandatory system be developed into reality, the possession of such territories will become, what it ought to be, a "white man's burden" instead of a white man's profit; and then the states will not intrigue against one another in order to take up the burden. If otherwise, we are faced by the double risk of insurrections by the native peoples, and wars among their masters.

In conclusion, it is only just to say of the British that in their Imperial policy, for something like a century past, there has been a continuous pressure away from dominion and exploitation, to trustee-ship and self-government. The two policies continue to contend with one another, and it would be hazardous to say that the latter has finally prevailed over the former. The struggle has been fiercest over Ireland, and in the very latest years, the contradictions there, the oscillations between the one course and the other, have been such as have astonished and perplexed the world. In 1921 we were endeavouring to govern Ireland by murder and theft. In the same year we offered her a constitution as free as that of Australia. The offer may have come too late. But if, by good chance, it succeeds, we shall have solved a problem and done something to redeem a crime that has extended over seven centuries.

In India and in Egypt, in these last years, we have witnessed the same oscillations, violence alternating with concessions. But in both those cases the final trend has been towards self-government. If that movement should succeed, and establish itself, a very great step will have been taken towards the stable peace of the world. But one thing should be clear. If we cannot govern people without massacring them, then we ought to go, and leave them alone. For Empire has no justification, unless the people governed are content with it, and unless it leads to, and is willing in the end to grant, self-government, within the scope and restraints of a League of Nations. I will add, to emphasise my point, that if the constitution granted to Ireland fails to come into effect, through the obstinate resistance of a great section of the Irish nation, then we ought not to intervene by force to impose it, or to impose some more autocratic form of British Government. We ought to refer the whole question to the League of Nations, and accept the decision of that body. The Irish were ready to do that in 1918. We refused. Have not events proved that we were wrong?

22

At this point I may close my argument, for any further elaboration of it would lead into a number of special problems and a mass of detail. But none of these can be fruitfully approached, still less settled, until we have decided whether we intend to have a world with war or without it. The main object will determine all the minor objects, and the general policy the policy in detail. I do not believe it to be possible any longer to halt between two opinions, to want to abolish war, and yet to prepare for it, to want liberty and yet to impose Empire, to want civilisation, and yet to cheat, steal and murder. I am not pretending that, at the best, we have before us an easy task or a certainty of salvation; but I am sure that, until we face the main issue and come out wholeheartedly for the abolition of war, we cannot move a step on the road to security. I have given my reasons for this belief as clearly as I can, and I do not see that any further elaboration could strengthen them. In one sense, the case is very simple, complex though it becomes as soon as a general truth begins to be applied to special cases.

Do you accept the general truth? That is the question I am putting to you. If you do not, do you know why? And are you prepared to defend your position? In the course of my book I have, I daresay, been provocative, without intending it; but I have had only one purpose, to force the attention of busy indifferent men upon the tremendous issue that faces us. I apologise freely and gladly beforehand for any imperfections in my manner of presenting the case; but I am sure that the case is there. I am sure that I am dealing with reality, and with terrible reality. I am sure that you, and all of us, are concerned. I ask you to put aside any irritation you may feel with me, and concentrate your thoughts on the tremendous question. Which is it to be?

Notes

Notes for
The Causes of International War

1. "As long as a nomad horde finds sufficient room in the steppe it does not think of migration and always returns home from its raids richly laden with plunder. But if the steppe-zone is thrown into a ferment by struggles for the winter pastures, or by other causes, the relatively weakest horde gets pushed out of the steppe and must conquer a new home outside the zone. For it is only weak against the remaining nomad hordes, but against any other state upon which it falls it is irresistible. All the nomads of history who broke into Europe, the Scythians, Sarmatians, Huns, Bulgarians, Avars, Magyars, Cumans, were the weakest in the steppes and had to take to flight, whence they became assailants of the world, before whom the strongest tottered." – *Cambridge Medieval History*, Vol. 1, p. 349

2. Mr. W. H. PERRY has put forward the rather sensational view that the very beginning of war was the conquest of peaceful peoples by adventurers bent on gold, pearls and amber, and on servile labour to produce them. On that hypothesis all war would be in the modern sense "imperialistic." See reference in the bibliography to Mr. Perry's very interesting paper. If his view were established it would more than ever show plunder as the root of war.

3. For the sake of clearness I have not paused in this place to draw the important distinction between a state and a nation, but write as though all the citizens of a state shared in the patriotism of it. This is not true, in the case of "empires" where some of the citizens belong to a nationaliy retained inside the state against its will, like the Egyptians or the Irish in the British Empire, or the Germans in the new Czecho-Slovak state.

4. This word "honour" has recently been discussed by an American writer, LEO PERLA, in a volume entitled *What Is National Honour?* (Macmillan, 1918). He has brought together a long list of passages where the word is used by patriots and statesmen. And the reader will find, if he turns to them, that there is hardly a case where "honour" means anything except power or (what is regarded as the outwork of power) prestige. On national honour see also VEBLEN: *On the Nature of Peace*, p.27ff

5. M. VENIZELOS cited in OAKES AND MOWATT: *The Great European Treaties of the Nineteenth Century*, p. 112

6. Cited in *Foreign Affairs*, April 1920, p. 2

7. June 1920

8. JOSEPH CAILLAUX: *Ma Politique Extérieure*, p. 6

9. And what that means may be gathered from the following account by Henri Barbusse: "We know the methods adopted to fetch them out of their own country. We know how they have been torn from their natural life by armed raids and incendiary fires, to be carried off into captivity and thrust into barracks, to be slaughtered by being used in attacks made in open country where masses of them perish, to die of cold and of diseases, which they did the more easily since their suffering awakened no echoes and they themselves hardly knew how to explain their troubles.

"How many – while I was at the front – have I not seen die of consumption, exhaustion, and melancholy, poisoned by our northern fogs, collapsing little by little like mere things, deprived of that southern sun which they needed.

"On the Riviera, where the rich enjoy all the subtleties of luxury and live princely lives, I have seen these unhappy blacks herded like animals in a pen. The arms of many of them were marked by weals from the ropes with which they had been tied to bring them from their country and to prevent them, once landed in Europe, from running away. Many of them committed suicide from wretchedness and through pining for their own land.

"All this has not prevented the pernicious Jingo Press from exalting the heroism of the traders in black flesh, whose energies had secured this additional number of soldiers for the home country, or from lavishing praise upon the clever manoeuvres which enabled us to benefit from the sacrifice of the black troops."

From a letter in *Foreign Affairs*, June 1920 – Special Supplement, p. 8

10. General Smuts, who took part in drawing up the Peace Treaties, has referred to the Peace Conference as a "seething cauldron of human greed and passion." Lord Robert Cecil has said: "Anyone who has had any personal experience of that strange body will desire anything rather than a renewal of its deliberations." (Hansard, H.C., 14th April 1920, v. 127, p. 1747).

Against the judgment passed in the text on the Peace Treaties it may be objected that no account has been taken of the Covenant of the League. That is for a reason. We are concerned here with causes of war, and therefore, with the evidence, only too conspicuous, that the purposes and ideas that cause war are still operative in the minds of statesmen and their nations. That there are signs of a reaction against these purposes and ideas, is a principal hope for the future, and the most notable sign is the Covenant of the League.

11. It is generally agreed that air-raids on cities will be a principal feature of the next war. And air-raids do not select for slaughter soldiers or male adults.

12. In the year 1913, the British exports to the whole of British tropical Africa (Somaliland, East Africa, Uganda, Nyassaland, Gambia, the Gold Coast, Sierra Leone, and Nigeria) were one per cent, of the whole, and the imports from those territories less than one per cent. Our trade with India, of course, is important. But who can do the sum which consists in calculating the expense of the long series of wars we have waged to secure our communications with India, against the hypothetical diminution of our trade with that country,

if it were occupied by a State protecting against us? The self-governing Dominions do not come into this argument. But it is very questionable whether we should do less trade with them, if they were not part of the British Empire.

13. Article 22, says, referring to the Turkish territories, "the wishes of these communities must be a principal consideration in the selection of the mandatory state." The Arabs of Mesopotamia and of Syria are showing, in the most conclusive way they can, that is by armed resistance, that they do not want the English nor the French. The latter indeed, at the moment of this writing, have sent an ultimatum to the Syrian Arabs, demanding that they accept the French as their mandatory under threat of war. Thus do governments interpret their obligations. This governmental cynicism and duplicity is so profound and so much a matter of course, that people hardly even attend to it. Yet it has already gone far to destroy the promise of the League of Nations, and to ruin the future peace of the world.

14. The wording of Article 22 is deplorably and perhaps purposely ambiguous. Thus it can, and probably will, be maintained that the words quoted in the text apply only to African territory and not to Asiatic. In that case the British and the French would not be breaking the letter of the Covenant if they established in the territories of the late Turkish Empire a trading and commercial monopoly. But they would none the less be infringing the spirit. For the object of the Covenant is to prevent war, and a principal cause of war is the creation of such exclusive national privileges.

If territories seized by one state are to be closed economically to others, then states are bound to fight for territories rich in industrial resources. The same observation applies to the case of the island of Nauru referred to below. It is open to the British to say (as they have done) that this mandate is held under the sixth clause of Article 22, and that therefore the condition of equal commercial opportunity does not apply to it. None the less, the action they have taken is a breach of the spirit of the Covenant.

15. See Hansard, vol. 130, No. 78, p. 1337

16. The British are maintaining in Mesopotamia a force of 80,000 troops at an estimated cost of at least £35,000 per annum. All this we can do in our own supposed interest. But we cannot spare a man or a shilling to save the Armenians from massacre – we who have "troubled deaf heaven with our bootless cries," again and again, on this subject, and have made it a special count against the Germans that they did not stop the massacres at a time when they had no troops in the Turkish Empire, and no possibility of taking any there.

Notes for
War: Its Nature, Cause and Cure

17. See *Nation*, July 21, 1921

18. Cited by Mr. PONSONBY in the U.D.C. for September 1917

19. *Labour Leader*, October 19, 1916. As the dates are not given, I have not been able to verify these extracts, but I see no reason to doubt their correctness. And even if not correct they would be *bien trouvés*.

20. *Causes of International War* (George Allen and Unwin, Ltd.)

21. This seems to be probable. But it is possible that the general mobilisation (as distinguished from that against Austria) was not ordered before the 30th. The point is not of great importance to our purpose.

22. PRINCE SIXTE OF BOURBON: *Austria's Peace Offer*. Edited by MANTEYER.

23. Ibid. p. 99

24. Ibid. p. 103

25. Ibid. p, 173

26. Ibid. p. 174

27. Ibid. p. 28

28. Ibid. p. 173

29. Ibid. p. 28

30. Ibid. p. 139

31. Ibid. p. 126

32. Ibid. p. 178

33. *Disenchantment*, by C. E. MONTAGUE

34. BARON S. A. KORFF: *Russia's Foreign Relations*, p. 45

35. Now (November 1932) said to be withdrawn.

36. Now settled in the sense that the straits are to be free to war-ships; settled, that it, with a view to having a next war.

37. See *What Really Happened at Paris*, ed. by E. M. HOUSE and C. SEYMOUR. Chapter on Reparations, by T. W. LAMONT.

38. FRANK ARTHUR VANDERLIP: *What Next in Europe?*, p. 66 (George Allen and Unwin, Ltd.)

39. This sentence perhaps does Mr. Lloyd George injustice. For he has since explained that he always intended that Germany should pay for pensions.

40. Now, November 1922, abandoned.

41. Written before the election of 1922 in England.

42. FRANCIS DELAISI: *Oil*, p.28 (George Allen and Unwin, Ltd.).

43. The *fascisti* have now, by armed revolution, seized power for themselves. This is what the Bolshevists did in Russia.

A Short Bibliography

From *Causes of International War*

The confirmation of the position taken in the text is to be sought in all history past and contemporary. For the convenience of the reader who wishes to pursue the matter, a short list of books is here added.

Chapter 1

WILLIAM TROTTER: *Instincts of the Herd in Peace and War*, (Fisher Unwin, 1916)

Chapter 2

HAVELOCK ELLIS: *Is War Diminishing?* in *Essays in War Time* (Constable, 1916), and *The Origin of War* in *The Philosophy of Conflict and other Essays in War Time* (Constable, 1919)

RUDOLF HOLSTI: *The Relation of War to the Origin of the State* (Helsingfors, 1913)

W. J. PERRY: *War and Civilisation* in *Bulletin of the John Ryland's Library*, Manchester, Vol. IV., Nos. 3 and 4, February and July 1918.

J. L. MYRES: *The Dawn of History* in *The Home University Library* (Williams and Norgate)

Chapter 3

GOLDSWORTHY LOWES DICKINSON: *The European Anarchy* (George Allen and Unwin, 1916)

H. E. EGERTON: *British Foreign Policy in Europe to the End of the Nineteenth Century.* (Macmillan and Co., 1917)

A. MOWATT OAKES, K.B.: *The Great European Treaties of the Nineteenth Century* (Oxford. Clar. Press, 1918)

LEO PERLA: *What is National Honour?* (Macmillan, 1918)

W. G. F. PHILLIMORE: *Three Centuries of Treaties of Peace* (John Murray, 1917)

L. S. WOOLF: *Empire and Commerce in Africa* (George Allen and Unwin), and *Economic Imperialism*, in the *Swarthmore International Handbooks* (Swarthmore Press)

Chapter 4

GOLDSWORTHY LOWES DICKINSON: *The Choice Before Us* (Allen and Unwin, 1917)

THORSTEIN VEBLEN: *An Inquiry into the nature of Peace and the Terms of its Perpetuation* (Macmillan and Co., 1917)

www.ingramcontent.com/pod-product-compliance
Lightning Source LLC
Chambersburg PA
CBHW020319010526
44107CB00054B/1901